Praise for

Deliberately DIFFERENT

"In *Deliberately Different*, Judee von Seldeneck and Aileen Alexander deliver an inspiring and decisive guide to navigating cross-generational leadership. In this book, their commitment to mentoring and paying it forward demonstrates the quintessential definition of knowing their value!"

> MIKA BRZEZINSKI, co-host, *Morning Joe*, and founder of Know Your Value

"This book is a masterclass in leadership evolution, delivered with sharp insight and foresight by Judee von Seldeneck and Aileen Alexander, two of the most astute observers on the topic today. This book doesn't just explore leadership change—it equips you to lead it."

> DAVID L. COHEN, US ambassador to Canada and former senior executive vice president, Comcast Corporation

"Now more than ever, the world is desperate for good leadership. Whether you direct a nonprofit focused on social justice or you're a C-suite executive at the head of a Fortune 100 company, you need the incredible insights from this conversation between two of the world's top multidimensional leaders, so that you learn how to lead with integrity, practice effective strategy, and adapt easily to innovation."

> MEL ROBBINS, *New York Times* bestselling author and award-winning host of *The Mel Robbins Podcast*

"In navigating the complexities of modern business, understanding CEO succession, executive leadership development, and strategic Diversity and Inclusion consulting is crucial. *Deliberately Different* eloquently captures these elements through the insights of Judee von Seldeneck and Aileen K. Alexander. Their compelling road map makes this book an indispensable resource for leaders committed to fostering inclusive and dynamic leadership."

> MICHAEL C. HYTER, president and CEO of The Executive Leadership Council (ELC)

"Serving in the military, whether for four years or forty, instills leadership at the deepest level, shaping how you navigate every challenge in life. This book brilliantly captures the timeless leadership principles honed in service, offering lessons learned that could apply to the battlefield, the boardroom, and beyond."

> TOM C. SEAMANDS, Lt. General, US Army (retired)

Deliberately Different

www.amplifypublishinggroup.com

Deliberately Different: Fifty Years. Two Generations. Leading in a Changing World.

©2024 Diversified Search Group. All Rights Reserved. No part of this publication may be reproduced, stored in a retrieval system or transmitted in any form by any means electronic, mechanical, or photocopying, recording or otherwise without the permission of the author.

For more information, please contact:
Amplify Publishing, an imprint of Amplify Publishing Group
620 Herndon Parkway, Suite 220
Herndon, VA 20170
info@amplifypublishing.com

Library of Congress Control Number: 2024917865

CPSIA Code: PRV0924A

ISBN-13: 979-8-89138-292-3

Printed in the United States

To the leaders who have inspired us and to the visionaries who will lead the way for generations to come. This book is for you.

Deliberately
DIFFERENT

Fifty Years. Two Generations.
Leading in a Changing World.

JUDITH M. VON SELDENECK
AND AILEEN K. ALEXANDER

Contents

Introduction   1

PART 1
Our Take on Timeless Leadership Qualities

CHAPTER 1
Using Your Strengths   15

CHAPTER 2
Embracing the Challenges   43

CHAPTER 3
The Confidence to Take Risks   57

PART 2
Essential Traits for the Modern Leader

CHAPTER 4
The Art of Reading the Room   81

CHAPTER 5
It's All about Your People   97

CHAPTER 6
You're Not Given Power; You Earn It!   111

EPILOGUE
Being Deliberately Different:
Leading into the Future   133

Acknowledgments   145

About the Authors   151

Introduction

The world is changing faster than ever before. And that rapid rate of change means that the expectations for modern leaders have become vast and varied. No matter the arena, we expect today's leaders to communicate openly and with total transparency, take stands on key issues, and drive performance in an ever-evolving, complex, interconnected, and deeply polarized environment.

But in the midst of all that change, a few things have stayed the same, including the fundamental need for leadership. No technology, not even AI, can replace the human dimensions of leadership that have stood the test of time. Regardless of the decade, the geography, and the industry, some elements have persevered: leaders operate with integrity and character, they take risks and are willing to learn from failures. They take responsibility and accountability for missteps and shortcomings, but always share their success with their teams. Great leaders are great communicators who embody listening and take honest feedback to heart. They see that great leadership is always about reaching current business and team goals and also about the future. Leaders with true staying power are still the ones who take care of their people, always, knowing that doing so will help take care of the organization's ultimate goals.

These qualities show up in accomplished individuals of all types and stripes, across time and across sectors. We know this because we've been fortunate enough to have front-row seats to multiple arenas of leadership, having spent time in politics, the military, philanthropy, and business. And the work we do now—in executive search and transformational leadership advisory at Diversified Search Group (DSG)—affords us the privilege and opportunity to advise and guide C-suite executives, nonprofit directors, academic department heads, startup founders, operating partners, and other mavericks. Through that wealth of exposure and experience, we've been observing and assessing leaders for decades, taking careful notes, and seeing how important these behaviors (among a handful of others) have remained relevant.

And as we've observed and assessed, we've also tried to live up to, embrace, or embody those qualities ourselves. It's an ongoing journey, to be sure.

We began our careers at very different times and in very different places. Judee started out in Washington, DC, during the Civil Rights Movement of the 1960s, and Aileen in the military on the heels of 9/11. Judee made the leap into entrepreneurship fairly early on, while Aileen learned the inner workings of the public sector from the inside out. Each of us was fortunate enough to work for and alongside great leaders, and to learn from how they operated. And our work at DSG enables us to continue in that vein, counseling and learning from multiple leaders across multiple industries.

Introduction   3

The two of us have evolved in different ways and adopted different leadership styles, but we maintain many of the same core principles. We seem like polar opposites, and in some ways, we are—but in others, we are perfectly and completely aligned.

The stories we'll share with you in these pages follow us both along our paths, noting where we've diverged and where we've intersected. We've each found success in our own ways and in our own times. Learning and growing as we go.

Judee had to bust through barriers. In the 1970s when she founded DSG, executive search was a $100-million-a-year industry with fewer than a dozen major players.[1] (By comparison, it's now a $25 billion industry, and the United States alone has 5,630 executive search businesses.[2]) At that time, women could not take out business loans under their own names,[3] and by 1972, only one woman had ever made it onto the Fortune 500 CEO list (Katharine Graham, who led the *Washington Post* from 1963 to 1991 and was CEO of the Washington Post Company).[4]

All this meant Judee had an uphill battle to fight, and she did so with her characteristic mix of charm, grit, business acumen, and innovation. The firm's growth was steady for decades, but ten years ago, Judee identified a way to access capital, which historically was

---

[1] https://www.nytimes.com/1974/08/11/archives/trophies-of-the-headhunters-trophies-of-the-headhunters.html

[2] https://www.ibisworld.com/industry-statistics/number-of-businesses/executive-search-recruiters-united-states

[3] https://www.forbes.com/sites/deborahsweeney/2018/08/21/how-hr-5050-changed-entrepreneurship-for-women/?sh=836457011a55

[4] https://fisher.osu.edu/blogs/leadreadtoday/a-brief-history-female-fortune-500-ceos

not open to women. She partnered with a private equity firm—and was one of the first in the industry to do so—which enabled the company to acquire several other boutique firms and grow exponentially. Along the way, she continued to open doors and break barriers. In 2013, Judee named Dale E. Jones to be president and CEO of Diversified Search, and for the next decade, they led the firm through unprecedented growth and expanded the firm's corporate and board practices. Notably, Dale was the only Black man to lead one of the top ten executive search firms in the country. Five decades after Judee started with a small executive search company, Diversified Search Group was widely recognized as one of the top firms in the industry.

Aileen grew up and came of age in the 1980s and '90s, and saw a world where Title IX had been in place for decades and women leaders were on the rise. By 1997, women CEOs ran six of the Fortune 500 companies,[5] and fifty-seven women were serving in the US Congress.[6] Even in her younger years, Aileen was aware of the pieces of the glass ceiling the previous generation had shattered. She felt it was her generation's responsibility to lower a rope ladder to the leaders coming up behind her. During the 1990s and 2000s, Aileen's path took her through Army Reserve Officers' Training Corps (ROTC) at Johns Hopkins University, Harvard Kennedy School, the US Army, the Department of Defense, Capitol Hill, and the private industry. During this time, she watched and learned from national leaders across disciplines and tried to hone her own

---

[5] https://www.catalyst.org/wp-content/uploads/2019/05/ Catalyst_Women_Fortune_CEOs_1972-2019_Historical_List_5.16.2019.pdf

[6] https://cawp.rutgers.edu/facts/levels-office/congress/history-women-us-congress

brand of bold-yet-flexible leadership rooted in service, trust, and adaptability.

We are just two leaders among many, and we have such different styles, different strengths, and different approaches. But what we have in common is a willingness to pursue our North Star. A drive to be Deliberately Different as leaders, to break from the pack in thoughtful and strategic ways—at times when doing so will have the most positive impact. We fully agree with what Bill George wrote in his seminal book *True North*, that "successful leadership takes conscious development and requires being true to your life story." We rely on our past observations and experiences, but aren't afraid to evolve, change, and grow. (Perfect example: at age eighty-four, Judee is mastering LinkedIn, while GenXer Aileen, at age forty-eight, is diving into the world of generative AI tools.) We've both taken roads less traveled, taken swings (and struck out on occasion), taken stands grounded in our values, and made bets on others and ourselves. We try to stay humble, but we're also not afraid to stand out.

Our positions at DSG have given us amazing opportunities to see how leadership has evolved, how new roles have emerged while others have been sunset, and how nonlinear paths have become the new norm. We've noted how access to leadership positions has changed dramatically over the past decades—not just for women leaders but for all leaders—and how the circumstances in which leaders must lead have changed and will continue to do so. But we've also observed that certain timeless leadership traits are always part of the equation. Every time. And we hope this book will help you see those qualities in yourself and in others.

We also hope you'll read our stories and learn to discount the idea that simply working harder, longer, or more intensely is likely to lead to success and fulfillment. In our view, it's not about leaning in; it's about *getting* in (and staying in the room where it's all happening). It's about being attuned to the circumstances and environment, illustrating the intelligence and value you bring, and finding a way to make inroads. Sometimes that takes grit, sometimes it takes patience, sometimes it's about listening, and sometimes it's about finding the right allies, sponsors, and advocates. But fundamentally, getting yourself into the right rooms and securing seats at the right tables comes from honing your skills, leveraging your power, using your voice to add value to the conversation, and cultivating the belief that you belong, even when imposter syndrome seeps in. Leaders also have the responsibility to invite varied perspectives and diverse experiences to the table and create conditions where everyone is encouraged to be themselves and reach their potential.

This approach is not only an effective way to get things done but also ensures you're in the room, influencing key decisions.

Judee: Tell them about Little League.

Aileen: Now?

Judee: Yes, now! Are you kidding? This is the perfect spot for that story.

Aileen: I suppose it's relevant here. All right, here goes.

Introduction 7

I've always loved sports and been super competitive. And thankfully, my parents were incredibly supportive since I insisted on trying just about every sport under the sun. When I was about eight years old, I played on a coed Little League team, which I absolutely loved. My family was spending our summers at my nana's house in a small beach town on Long Island, New York, and I remember the smell of the ocean. Though when it came to the baseball field, I recall the smell of fresh-cut grass, the gritty texture of dirt mixed with sand, the feeling of an oversized, broken-in baseball glove that was way too big for my hand. It was a wonderful place to spend my summer afternoons.

There was just one problem: the tee.

The league gave the boys the choice to hit off the pitch or a tee, but made all of the girls hit off of a tee. The only other girl on the team was perfectly comfortable with this arrangement, but I was livid. It wasn't so much that I wanted to show up the boys; it was about making sure I had a choice, and proving to myself that I could play at their level. And here I was, stuck in a rigged system that didn't even give me a chance!

After practice, I hopped on my banana-seat bike and pedaled as fast as I could back to my nana's house to tell my family about this unfair rule. My parents were a little nonplussed, but my nana met my outrage with her own.

"Does that seem right to you, Aileen?" she asked.

"No!" I said, brows furrowed.

"And are you going to let them get away with it?"

I grinned up at her and said, "No way."

When I stepped up to bat at my very first game, the coach immediately dragged the tee out and set it on home plate. I waited until he'd backed off and settled down on the bench to watch the action, then dragged it away, off to the side of the catcher's box. As I approached the plate again, bat in hand, he scrambled back off of his bench and replaced the tee, glowering at me a little as he did it. And, as you might've guessed by now, I gave him a minute to settle back down into his seat, then hauled the contraption away. The coach threw up his hands in defeat while my entire family scream-cheered from the bleachers.

Then I watched as the outfielders came creeping in, fully expecting me to, well, hit like a girl.

I missed the first pitch, fouled the second, and by that time I was absolutely determined to at least get myself onto first base. The third pitch came in true, and I swung with every ounce of my might. That ball sailed over those doubting outfielders and hit the back fence. I stood there at home plate, happy but unsure what to do next, while my parents yelled at me to start running the bases. So I did. Until I'd rounded them all.

It felt good to make the other team regret underestimating me, but again, I mostly just wanted to prove to myself that I could do this. I didn't need coddling or special treatment; I knew my capabilities, and I wanted options. I also wanted to be challenged. To do hard things and get better at them.

So with encouragement and support, I handled the situation in a way that didn't allow anyone to hold me back. I did what I needed to do to prove that I belonged.

Judee: I just adore that story. So, did that coach try to drag the tee out for you ever again?

Aileen: Nope. And he never mentioned it either. To me or my parents.

Judee: Good!

Aileen: But I didn't stick with baseball, as you know. I tried other sports, including basketball. Though I got cut from the grade school team, and it just devastated me. That was awful. First team I ever tried out for, and I got cut.

Judee: Now hang on, I thought you played basketball in college.

Aileen: I did! You're right, and it's amazing to think about what's happening with women's basketball today. In my own experience, getting cut early on just made me more determined to put in the extra work and effort to get better, make the next team, and be valuable to them.

Judee: That sounds like you, all right.

Aileen: Yeah, I absolutely love team play. Winning, losing, just being part of a group that's working together and pooling their talents. And you, Judee, have assembled and been on some world-class teams yourself …

Judee: Well, thank you. But you know what? Let's tell them about that later on.

Sometimes earning your seat at the table really is as simple as dragging that tee off of home plate. Sometimes it's more complicated and nuanced than that. Especially now, when business and workplace norms are at a critical inflection point.

But the two of us believe far too few people see that refusing to hit off the tee is even an option. It's time to shift that dynamic. We can't let ourselves get shoved into boxes, accept pre-made identities, or assume that busting out of them is impossible. No more being sold a bill of goods about our own capabilities. And as leaders, we also have a responsibility to challenge the rules and ensure that all have an equal and equitable opportunity to take a swing.

Learning to enter, read, and rule the room will look different for every single person in this world. Learning to bring your entire, authentic self to the leadership table is something we should all aspire to and have the opportunity to do. Unfortunately, that's not always the case. It is the leader's responsibility to create the conditions where everyone can thrive, fostering an environment that celebrates differences. Each of us must then have the willingness and confidence to embrace our uniqueness and contribute fully.

So we're going to spend the pages of this book sharing some of our own experiences with infiltrating rooms of importance and learning from what we saw take place inside. We've both rubbed elbows with some extraordinary people and accomplished a few noteworthy things, but we don't think of ourselves as being fancy, special, exceptional people. Still, our accomplishments give us credibility, and we've gained the respect of other leaders around us, purposefully and strategically. We know that we want to be included, to be heard. We want to contribute and lead. We want to have our say in the reframing of accomplishment and success. We want everyone to have a chance to take a swing.

Expectations for modern leaders have become vast and varied, and will no doubt continue to evolve. But between the two of us, we've had courtside seats to its evolution for nearly five decades, and observed that throughout the shifts and readjustments, a few key characteristics, behaviors, and beliefs remain unchanged. We're excited to share what we've learned, and hope it inspires you to drag a tee off your own home plate, somewhere, somehow, someday.

Part 1

OUR TAKE ON TIMELESS LEADERSHIP QUALITIES

Chapter 1

Using Your Strengths

I was there in 1963 when Dr. Martin Luther King Jr. told the world, "I have a dream." And did he ever!

Caught up in a sea of humanity—everyone hushed and reverent as the bright August sunshine beat down on the Lincoln Memorial—the crowd stood in awe while Dr. King delivered his impassioned, riveting speech as only a Southern Baptist minister could do. He roused the crowd of some 250,000 people to the famous chanting, "We shall overcome" and "Free at last, free at last, thank God almighty, we are free at last!" It felt like a movement was happening, like this showing of unity against our country's social wrongs could be a real turning point. And indeed it was.

That amazing day was only a year and a half after I'd moved to Washington to begin my post-college life. In 1962, after graduating from the University of North Carolina at Chapel Hill, I watched as all of my beloved sorority sisters went to Atlanta to teach school and find husbands. Being a political science major (just like Aileen),

I decided to take a different path: one that led me to Washington, DC, where John F. Kennedy had become president. It was a magical time in the nation's capital, often referred to as Camelot. Working in the US Senate was an honor and privilege! It allowed me to observe some great leaders in action, accumulating knowledge about others and learning on the job.

My first job was as a typist in the secretarial pool at the Department of Commerce (which was also home to the first iteration of the National Aquarium, just us typists and a bunch of freshwater fish, hanging out in the basement of the Herbert C. Hoover Building). I spent a year in this role—making a whopping $3,800 salary—then landed a secretarial job through a friend at Aerojet General, a defense contractor. I stayed there for another few years before my life-changing job came along: working for newly appointed Senator Walter Mondale, a Democrat from Minnesota.

The mid-1960s was an unprecedented period of time, with the extremely controversial war in Vietnam disrupting the country, and the Civil Rights Movement sparking demonstrations. There was strong emotion around both of these events. For me—having grown up in the South, where discrimination was everywhere and accepted as a way of life—it became a huge issue. For instance, our local drug store in High Point, North Carolina, posted signs that read "whites only," and Black people (or "coloreds" as they were referred to then) had to sit in the back of buses.

I knew that Walter F. Mondale was part of a group of senators like Bobby Kennedy, Fred Harris, and Birch Bayh, who came to the Senate in 1964 to make waves. They would become powerful forces in our country's history, passing legislation that would begin to right so many of the wrongs that were causing unrest and inspiring protests. To get a job as a personal secretary to Senator Mondale and

Using Your Strengths

work with him as he began this historic phase of his political career was something I will never forget, and it had a profound effect on me. I also believed at the time I was the youngest personal secretary to a US Senator, and my boyfriend was deputy press secretary to the president of the United States. I got to see the workings of government, both from the executive branch and the legislative branch.

I came of age in a time and place of massive change. I was there, in person, and saw up front and close, events that rocked the world.

While I was living and working in Washington, DC, President Kennedy, Dr. Martin Luther King Jr., and Senator Robert Kennedy were all assassinated, and all within a few years of each other. I marched in all of their funerals and many demonstrations. To this day, I'm deeply passionate about discrimination: I can feel it in an instant when it is occurring. I've made some enemies along the way for being a little too outspoken about it, but it's a deal-breaker for me.

Early on, I learned how to make my way while still holding on to my core principles and values. I love going against the grain—being Deliberately Different very much on purpose—and over the years, I've been fortunate to learn by experience the right way and the wrong way to do it. I admire people who have a balance of rebellion and diplomacy, and believe this balance is critical in terms of being an effective and inspiring leader.

Aileen: Yep, that's you, all right.

Judee: You, too, in your own way, Aileen. My voice may be a little louder and more strident, but I've watched you be a dissenting voice several times. And in some tough situations.

Aileen: I'm definitely willing to speak out when I need to. Especially when I can do it on behalf of people I know are struggling to be heard. I admire leaders who use their clout to support others … so I try to be one of them myself.

Judee: I know you do. That's something we have in common. Different tactics, same goal.

Aileen: Not sure I'd call myself an actual rebel, though.

Judee: Hmm. How about a rebel in spirit?

Aileen: I can go with that. As much as I can, I hope to use my own power and courage to do my part in building a more equitable and just society.

Power and courage.

Both are crucial to success in business, politics, sports … just about every area of life. Without power, a person in charge will struggle to be heard, to exert influence, and to drive their endeavor forward. Without courage to back it up, they won't have the endurance necessary to overcome obstacles.

"We can't understand leadership if we don't talk about power," says researcher and author Brené Brown. "In a 1968 speech given to striking sanitation workers in Memphis, Reverend Martin Luther King, Jr. defined power as the ability to achieve purpose and effect change. This is the most accurate and important definition of power

Using Your Strengths 19

that I've ever seen."[7] Brown also points out that unlocking courage requires us to walk through vulnerability, and that both power and courage should be underscored by self-awareness and resiliency.

We wholeheartedly agree, but would also add that power and courage are extremely variable. Many people think of them as brute forces, blunt instruments, and they certainly can be. But in the current climate, many leaders show their power by being innovative and flexible instead of single-minded and relentless. Many show their strength through generosity, curiosity, and inclusiveness. Others bring a strong vision to bear, then coach their people to enact it, or lead by making themselves the force that brings the best and brightest minds together to tackle tough problems. Power and courage drive *all* of these leadership styles in different ways and from different angles. People who inspire and lead in businesses, governments, communities, and families can win both hearts and minds using any one of these strategies. Or different ones in different situations.

We believe this because the two of us come from different generations, share different philosophies around motivating people, and lead in different ways—and we've both found what works for us. Judee is at her best when she's at the helm, sharing her vision and empowering her teams to bring it to fruition. Aileen excels when she can leverage both her own strengths and the strengths of her teammates, leading by identifying a strategically chosen North Star that unites and inspires everyone. As colleagues, we've learned so much from each other but also celebrate our differences.

---

[7] https://brenebrown.com/resources/brene-brown-on-power-and-leadership/

If our stories prove anything, it's that there is no single right way to lead. And if our experiences recruiting, advising, and coaching other leaders have taught us anything, it's that powerful people evolve over time with a growth mindset. The most gifted leaders we've known will pull different levers in different situations, and also allow themselves to grow and change over time. Anyone who characterizes themself too narrowly gets boxed in or boxed out. Flexibility and self-knowledge are equally valuable, with power and courage as their underpinnings.

Whoever you may be, find a way to lead that works for you.

And if you're not sure how to do that, start by figuring out who you are; think deeply about how you obtain and use power to boost your self-esteem, which is critical for success. That's what we've tried to do ourselves, as you'll soon see.

Judee and I diverge in many ways, but we've also had some pretty astonishing overlapping experiences. The main one that comes to my mind is how we've both lived through major historic events—turning points that transformed us as individuals and reshaped the world around us. For Judee, this was working in Washington, DC, during the Civil Rights and Vietnam War eras.

In my case, I was serving on active duty with the US Army during the September 11 attacks.

I received my commission in 1998, the post–Cold War era, which was a period of peace-keeping operations and transformation. I was twenty-two years old at that time, and my military operational specialty (MOS) was a 25 alpha, which meant I went

Using Your Strengths   21

in as a second lieutenant in the Signal Corps. This branch of the army creates and manages communications and information systems, and I spent my first few months on active duty in Augusta, Georgia, at the Signal Corps school. That's where I and my fellow junior officers got our technical and leadership training before we received our station assignments. I was assigned to the First Cavalry Division and stationed at Fort Cavazos (formerly Fort Hood), which is the largest and most populated US military installation in the world.[8]

To this day, I can still remember waking up early in the morning, working out with my unit, whether going on long runs or doing circuits. The base hummed with activity as the sun rose, and I was never alone. We would all pause at the sound of reveille over the loudspeaker, an incredible moment of shared respect that I got to experience each day. And all of this created a profound feeling of belonging to something greater than myself.

As a junior officer, I wore multiple hats. First, I was a platoon leader, then I moved into a staff job as S1, which meant I was responsible for personnel and HR for the battalion. Next, I became an executive officer (XO), which meant I was the number two in command of a company. This rotation of roles was meant to give officers exposure to various aspects of the work the army did on a daily basis. Much like leaders today may move from sales to operational leadership, or try to gain experience across functions so they can truly understand businesses from the inside out, the army wanted its leaders-in-training to see the full picture. It was an incredible experience, and fundamental for me as a leader twenty-five years later.

---

[8] https://home.Army.mil/cavazos/

Eventually I moved into S4, which is responsible for logistics and supply; I was in this role when the towers were hit.

I'll never forget that day. I mean, nobody will … but I felt like the world before the towers came down was a *completely* different place than the world after. The impact was profound and immediate, prompting a swift reevaluation of international relations, security measures, and diplomatic strategies across the globe.

I had just returned home after a workout with the women's running team on base when the planes struck. I was in my kitchen with *The Today Show* on in the background. I was standing there with my bowl of cereal and watched as the first plane hit. Like so many people, I assumed it was just an accident at that point. But once the second plane hit the second tower, I knew we were under attack.

I had just been in New York myself the week before for Labor Day. In fact, I'd just flown by the World Trade Center—had just seen the Twin Towers standing on the Manhattan skyline. Like so many people, I had family and friends in New York, and I knew a number of people who were impacted or lost people. This was the first foreign attack on American soil since Pearl Harbor in 1941. Like so many, I was shaken to my core.

But no one had the luxury of time to mourn and reflect. When we went back on base that morning, everything had already shifted. Our unit had been in a training posture up until the attacks, working on exercises and drills—activities that were all about readiness. And then, all of a sudden, we found ourselves moving to a wartime posture.

The transformation was literally overnight. The day before, we'd been focused on nation-state issues that were centered on peacekeeping. The day after, we were thrust into discussions of terrorism, counterterrorism, and asymmetric threats. New language, new national security dangers, and within a month, a foreign campaign in the form of Operation Enduring Freedom. The entire US Armed Forces was shifting strategically, operationally, and organizationally. Everything morphing at once.

A single event—and one that took place in just a few hours—changed everything. It changed our sense of security at home and within the rest of the world. It changed my life and the lives of everyone around me.

There was a memorial service shortly after, and I remember crossing paths with a sergeant who was on her way back from the service. The days that followed were incredibly intense, with activity in full swing, but I remember very clearly a moment in front of the base's chapel. She and I looked at each other for a long moment, and exchanged salutes. Then we both teared up. It felt more significant than any salute I'd given or received before. The distillation of what it meant to serve one's country.

Not too long after, we worked closely with the US Air Force, and eventually deployed a portion of our unit in support of Operation Enduring Freedom. I was responsible for helping with logistics, supplies, and maintenance for that battalion, so I spent time working with both soldiers and aviators, where we worked as a cohesive team. Despite being from different services with different uniforms and different specialties, we had one mission. We realized rank was not an indicator of best solutions. It was a blur of activity, with teams cross-coordinating, making critical decisions, supporting each other, and working at a breakneck pace. It was a true team effort.

In the moment, I was *not* thinking about how all this would impact me as a leader, how observing friends and colleagues as they reacted and took action collectively would influence me in years to come. In hindsight, however, it was one of the more formative events in my career. The leaders and soldiers around me—many of whom are still serving today—demonstrated the importance of persistence and keeping a cool head in the midst of chaos. I saw them working steadily and operating calmly, and noted how much that helped the soldiers they led. By setting the tone, these leaders encouraged their people to follow suit.

This is a perspective that I would return to in other moments throughout my career, and I'm so grateful to them for having shown me this example. In fact, I've sometimes been the one who steps in to help create order when massive change has taken root. It's served me well because after those attacks, the world revealed itself to be an increasingly complex geopolitical environment. Like so many others, I hadn't realized how much I couldn't see, sense, or respond to until that tragedy pulled back the curtain.

And in the years that followed, we saw even more complexity emerge. There's more uncertainty than certainty. Terrorist activity, disruptions in the world economy, shifts in political alliances, new digital technologies that turned entire industries inside out, a catastrophic pandemic, ongoing supply chain issues … it's been nonstop transformation since that horrific day in September, with no sign of stabilization. Preparing myself to navigate that as a leader and help my teams do the same has been tough but entirely worthwhile.

Both Judee and I lived through unprecedented inflection points in our country's history, and those events shaped our leadership trajectories. She emerged with a renewed dedication to fighting discrimination and the ability to walk the line between defiance and diplomacy. I emerged with the ability to recognize uncertainty and navigate upheaval. My experience in the army and the US government honed my understanding of the valuable role leaders play in bringing order to chaos, especially in a world that is increasingly uncertain and interconnected.

Judee: I knew 9/11 had a profound impact on you, Aileen, but I didn't understand until more recently how pivotal it was for you as a leader.

Aileen: It changed me forever, to be sure. I learned the importance of being prepared, watching the leaders around me putting their training to work. We were all shocked and scared on the inside, but I saw those officers draw on deep reserves of calm to help their teams stay on an even keel and focus on the mission. It was extraordinary. And I do my best to emulate that cool-headedness myself now.

Judee: It can be tough to do, but I agree it's super important.

Aileen: All right, Judee, it's your turn now. You know I'm all about context, and we can't discuss owning our strengths without sharing some history and background from our early days. So let's dig into some of your accomplishments. Maybe you could talk about how visionary you were in founding DSG as a firm that placed women exclusively? Why don't you start with the red briefcase!

Judee: Hmm. Yeah, that could work as a starting point. All right, so a few years after I'd married Clay and moved to Philadelphia, I bought out a little staffing firm called Distaffers. They found work for women who wanted to split up their shifts; one would take the morning, the other the afternoon. It was all right, an interesting concept, but they weren't exactly making money hand over fist. And having just come from DC, where I'd been working in the thick of the Civil Rights Movement, I wanted to push the envelope a little farther. I was passionate about fighting discrimination. I was not a radical or a feminist out there burning my bra in rebellions, but I had strong passion and wanted to do my part in helping level the playing field. I bought out Distaffers, eventually changed the name of the company to Diversified Search, and we began placing women and minorities, as they were referred to in the '70s, in full-time professional roles in the five-county Philadelphia region.

Aileen: Which was a tall order in the early '70s, I'm sure.

Judee: Not as tall an order as you might think, actually. With the Civil Rights Act in 1964 and the Equal Employment Opportunity Commission getting started in 1965, there was a lot of pressure on companies who had government contracts to hire women back then. As it turned out, there were many qualified women holding down good jobs in the not-for-profits who could transition to comparable corporate roles.

Aileen: So you stepped in and filled an empty niche?

Judee: I guess you could say we did that. I mean, it wasn't all as strategic as we're making it sound; I was trying to figure out what to do with my life in terms of work, having left the excitement of working in the US Senate for almost ten years. I was convinced I could have it all: be a wife, mother, and a professional all at once. And fortunately, that happened!

Aileen: That sounds like breaking barriers to me …

Judee: That's not really how I saw it. I just wanted to be active, contribute, do what I could. Anyway, the business got rolling, and I was surprised by how much I enjoyed it. I even loved my commute. There was a local train, and in 1974, I was usually the only woman who'd be out on the platform with the men every morning, in my heels and skirt, holding my little red briefcase. They would look at me, these men, and I knew what they were thinking. They were thinking, "Poor Clay. How did he end up with her?"

Aileen: Pretty sure I know your answer … but did that make you feel self-conscious?

Judee: Oh, heck no! I loved being the only woman out there. I always loved being the only woman, especially in business settings. They couldn't miss me being there, and I always made it a point to speak up and hopefully add value.

Aileen: I bet you did. You've never been afraid to stand out. That's definitely one of your biggest strengths.

Judee: Funny, though, that so many powerful people nowadays seem afraid to stand out. Especially women. I see them toning themselves down and deferring to others. Where's the charisma? The pride? The confidence? The boldness? How can anyone expect to be successful if they hide their light under a bushel?

Aileen: Well, as we've said, the dynamics of power are shifting right now—and have already shifted to some extent. Post-pandemic, a whole bunch of leaders have had to change tactics. Some learned the hard way that they needed to become more transparent and adapt to multiple modes of communication or risk being ousted. Employees and teams now have new perspectives on their value and work in general, often influenced by multi-generational viewpoints. As a result, executives and other leaders have had to adapt.

Judee: I get that. I just think there's a fine line between being accommodating and being a wimp. I think no matter what the situation may be, you have to be authentic and not change to suit a situation.

Aileen: Agree you always need to be real, but I believe there are times when we need to make strategic shifts to meet emerging needs and expectations. New formats make a huge difference too. An all-hands meeting in person is a totally different animal from one over Zoom. The best leaders I've encountered are the ones who've learned from these new ways of connecting, and noted that different employees may absorb and process in different ways. Reflecting that may feel like a major philosophy change to some people, but it could also just be adjusting your style while staying real to suit the times, right?

Judee: Another fine line, in my opinion. And one I've watched you walk, Aileen. I do admire that in you, but it's not something I can do myself. I prefer to show my true nature—my personality and strengths and weaknesses—and let people decide how they'll align themselves.

Aileen: Which has worked for you from the very start, and I try to do the same.

In 1974, when Judee bought into Distaffers, a staffing firm for women to share jobs, workplace dynamics were different. The feminist and civil rights movements had forced companies to reconsider their hiring practices, but the new populations of incoming employees still faced biases and challenges. Women were increasingly able to work, but struggled for independence in other ways. For example, they couldn't get credit cards without their spouses' signatures. People of color were hired into more office environments, but seldom treated as equals. Women founders and CEOs were a rare breed, even rarer than they are today, when they make up approximately 10 percent of the global pool.[9] Progress was being made, but slowly. And those in power were the same folks who'd been at the top for decades.

---

[9] https://fortune.com/2023/08/02/fortune-global-500-female-ceos-women/

Getting into the right rooms and securing seats at the right tables was incredibly challenging for many aspiring leaders.

Over the next five decades, dynamics continued to shift, and people who'd been excluded from power positions gradually made their way into rooms where big decisions were made. Over that stretch of time, DSG became one of the top ten executive search firms in the country, and by 2022, when Aileen became CEO, the firm was poised to take our unique brand and approach to finding great leaders to the next level. It was a big challenge, not just because Aileen was the only woman leading a top firm in the industry, but because DSG had been through the acquisition of five boutique executive search and consulting firms in just five years. We were moving at pace with the changing world, and we needed to focus on integration of our people and our systems.

As the two of us began working together, it was important that we get to know each other, learn from each other, and figure out how to work successfully to grow our company even further. Again, as leaders who grew up in different eras, we knew we had different lessons and perspectives to share. We both love people and love learning, so we were eager to find out how we could collaborate to keep DSG on a path to continual success.

So, as Aileen was getting settled into the firm and not long before she was announced as the new CEO, we had an important dinner—with just each other. We spent a long evening just talking and sharing stories from our lives.

Using Your Strengths 31

Aileen: Oh, that was a fun night. We talked about our childhoods, our families ... had some great food and amazing wine.

Judee: We sure did. That dinner was a way for us to find out more about our backgrounds and get a sense of who we really are in terms of our values and what's important to us in life. And for me to make sure I'd hired the right person for the job.

Aileen: Ah, the truth comes out. You were still screening me!

Judee: I didn't make any secret of it. I mean, I wanted to have some fun with you, too ...

Aileen: Always.

Judee: Well, yeah. I try to make every business meeting fun, if I can. You learn a lot about people when they relax and feel comfortable. Humor is one of a leader's best tools, if you ask me.

Aileen: That's definitely one of your strengths. I've seen you make some deeply serious people laugh. It breaks the ice and gets them to trust you.

Judee: You can't take yourself too seriously and have the "big ego" syndrome and only talk about yourself. You want to focus on others, get them to relax with you and have an open and honest conversation. Anyhow, that night at the restaurant, I loved learning exactly how competitive you are, Aileen. That's something we have in common.

Aileen: Yes, though our competitiveness manifests in different ways. I think you should talk a bit more about yours.

Back in the early '70s, around the birth of the women's movement, I was watching Betty Friedan and Gloria Steinem take a very radical approach to civil rights. All that bra burning, the big demonstrations, it was really aggressive. Don't get me wrong, I'm forever grateful they did it because it *really* got people's attention. But that wasn't my approach. I felt like, for me, there was another route. And it was one I'd taken my whole life.

I grew up in High Point, North Carolina, with a salesman father, homemaker mother, a brother named Fred, and my sister, Incy. I was the oldest, always most comfortable being in charge. My childhood there was absolutely idyllic, let me tell you. High Point was gorgeous, a small-town neighborhood where everyone knew everyone. I spent hours talking on the phone and hanging out with my girlfriends. We would ride bikes all over. I tied ropes around the handlebars of my red Schwinn and pretended it was a horse. Called it Trigger, just like on *The Roy Rogers Show.*

I was athletic from the start because I enjoyed sports and loved being active. But I think it was also because I had this inkling that the boys had it better somehow. Everyone listened to them, did what they asked without question. I mean, I was the apple of my father's eye until my brother came along, and after that I had to jockey for his attention. Boys were always where the action was. Even as a little girl, I could tell that boys and men just had more power, more sway. I was more comfortable hanging out with

Using Your Strengths   33

them. I never did the "girl thing." I was considered a "tomboy." I don't think I ever owned a doll or played with dolls like my girl-friends did.

So I invited myself along, walked into the spaces where the boys were so I could *also* be where the action was.

Here's a great example: lots of the kids in the neighborhood would come around to our side yard to play football. Mostly my brother's friends. But because I was the oldest, I made myself the quarterback and, you know, sort of ran the whole thing. That worked just fine for me, and no one really complained. But then one day my mother came out and said, "Judee, would you please come inside?" Which I did. Then she said, "Let your brother be in charge, won't you? These are *his* friends. You shouldn't be out there bossing them around."

She didn't give me the old "unladylike" speech because she knew that wouldn't fly with me, but I was still irritated. I loved playing with the boys, even bossing them around a little. I didn't see any problem with being just as competitive as a boy, just as driven and athletic.

And that extended to non-sports stuff too. I won the contest in eighth grade for selling the most magazine subscriptions. I don't think kids do this anymore, but they used to have these things where you'd go door to door and sell subscriptions to raise money for your team or your club or whatever. I was bound and determined to win that thing, and sure enough, I did. I think wanting to win was just ingrained in me at a very early age, and I learned I was going to have to fight and stand my ground if I was going to get my way.

Well, I don't play a lot of football now, at my age, and my days as a door-to-door magazine subscription salesgirl are long over. But

I know that competitive gene is still well and alive, and I think it's a real asset. I see a lot of leaders, these days, kinda tiptoeing around contentious situations instead of diving right in, or if they are competitive, they sometimes do it in less obvious ways, less confrontational. I prefer to be direct but persuasive and gently firm. I try to never lose sight of the bottom line and the ultimate goal in the moment at hand. I'll pour a little honey on it—I am from the South, after all—but I'm not afraid to explain to anyone when they're full of it, or when I think I can do something better than a competitor. I can't let sleeping dogs lie, as they often say in the South.

Since we both work in executive search and consulting—recruiting and advising leaders in top positions across industries—we know quite well that competitiveness can be both a strength and a weakness. It all depends on the person and how they choose to manifest it. Some leaders are so driven by the need to win that it eclipses everything else about them, and that's a recipe for disaster. People can see right through this. In fact, we'd argue that's not even competitiveness anymore; it's more like aggression, a need for control, which may boost a company's bottom line initially but will end up hurting the culture and the leader's credibility. Transparency in leaders is part of the new definition of empowered leadership.

Our own drive to compete is rooted in who we are as individual leaders. Judee is an extrovert and likes to be in the thick of things. Some say her ability to engage and charm is her competitive advantage. Aileen is warm, friendly, and approachable but a self-admitted ambivert. She's energized by being around people but needs time

Using Your Strengths

to be alone and reflect. Her competitiveness stems from wanting to do her very best and shine as part of a team.

We're both highly competitive, but we each march to the beat of our own drummer.

In school, in sports, in the military, in my career ... I've always considered myself to be competitive. But I wasn't out to prove myself to others or even surpass them. I'm just one of those people who always wants to do her best, period.

But to be clear, I was never *the* best at anything. I wasn't so innately gifted that I could just float to the top in academics or sports; I had to work hard. All the time. And I was absolutely willing to do that because I enjoyed the push-pull feeling of competing against myself. Even as I got older and entered the workforce, it was about doing *my* best in the face of challenges.

That said, excelling as an individual wasn't nearly as compelling to me as winning alongside teammates. Team sports and activities have always been where I feel most at home. I loved the feeling of being part of a group that was working toward a shared goal. I was in student government in high school, and really enjoyed the dynamics of puzzling things out with the other kids. I was always starting clubs and projects, organizing events—and yeah, I'd put myself in charge of anything I pulled together! But my competitive side was more overt when I could flex it on behalf of my team. I never wanted to do my best at the expense of others, or ruin someone else's shot at success with my own ambitions. I was much happier if we all got what we wanted and needed together, when my win was also their win. The whole "high tide lifts all boats" philosophy really resonates with me.

I couldn't say for sure, but that urge to compete on behalf of a team may have come from the fact that my family moved around *a lot* when I was a kid. I consider myself originally from Philly—the land of perpetual underdogs—even though we've lived on both coasts and across the Midwest. Which had some benefits for sure: I became super close with my parents and brother, learned to be super adaptable, and got to live in the thick of a slew of American regional cultures. (Case in point: when we lived in California, I was mesmerized by surf culture. I wanted *so badly* to win an Ocean Pacific Surf competition, although I never surfed. But I could hold my own on a boogie board.)

But all that moving also meant I was the new kid at school every few years. And the quickest way to overcome that? Join a team, stage crew, a group, any endeavor that takes cooperation, and apply my desire to be part of a group and my competitive streak to our shared success.

My senior year of high school, my soccer team beat one of the top teams in the country. And believe me, we were *not* supposed to win. It was a total underdog story, one I'm convinced would make a phenomenal movie. Our coach was a former marine who had us playing in the boys' league during the summers, driving us hard. He wanted us all fully committed to the high school team. He held everyone accountable at every turn. I learned a lot from him about team versus individual, and it stuck. Hard lessons, but good ones.

The championship journey was an amazing one for my teammates and me. The long practices, tough games, roller-coaster ride of wins

Using Your Strengths

and close games … all of it drew us together. I was the goalkeeper, and I loved the feeling of defending that goal on behalf of my team. A photo of me and one of my teammates from that era actually ended up winning an award in our local paper. We'd gone into overtime, and my teammate scored the winning goal, so I ran across the field to her, and I was so jazzed that I picked her up by her legs and lifted her in the air. The photo is of the both of us, her looking down at me and me looking up at her, both grinning like maniacs. It perfectly captures who we were as a team: we were playing for each other.

I love being fully engaged with a group of people, all working toward the same goal; it's as simple as that. Winning as a team, losing as a team, that feeling of unity. And I say that having experienced every role. I was captain; I was a starter; I was on the bench cheering on my teammates. So I've learned what it means to know your role on the team.

We all play a role. And the very best leaders I've observed recognize and honor that.

Judee: Fascinating. You know, I am very much about supporting my people, but I actually think about it quite differently from you. It's not about "doing it for the team," though I certainly understand that sentiment. For me, it's more "Who's on the bus with me?" I want to know who's going to walk the walk with me, step up with me, get their hands dirty with me so we can prevail together.

Aileen: Have you always felt that way? Been like that?

Judee: I think so. You know me, I prefer to be in control. Always have. Maybe that's what goes into having a competitive personality.

Aileen: But if I remember right, your competitive streak didn't extend to academics.

Judee: Oh, you remember right. Studying was so boring to me. I would've rather been out riding my bike or playing sports or talking on the phone to my girlfriends. Everything about school felt inconsequential to me, like it had nothing to do with the real world.

Aileen: But you went to college and eventually law school, right?

Judee: Yes, though I never finished my law degree. I saw law school as a pathway to a professional career instead of being a secretary my whole life. I've always been ambitious, always eager to do big things. Did I ever tell you that when I was a little girl, I would go into my dad's office and pretend to be him?

Aileen: Seriously!? Did you really?

Judee: Oh yes. He was a big deal at 3M Company, and I would pick up the phone and talk like he did when he was on a business call. And somehow, some of me prattling on got recorded, so we had a record of me pretending to be my own dad! Anyhow, I think I did that because some part of me wanted to be like him. Important, powerful, decisive.

Aileen: I love that so much.

Judee: Even at age five or six, I knew that men had it better than women. It seemed men were getting more advantages than women. I've always struggled with that. I don't mind people being valued because of what they've accomplished or how they present themselves, but just because you're a man? I never could quite get comfortable with that on any level.

Aileen: So, given that you became a woman CEO in an era when so few women ran their own companies, how did you navigate those gender issues at the time?

My strategy was to get the boys to like me so I could have a seat at the table. If I gained their trust and friendship, and they liked me, then we could joke and talk about sports. That seemed to put them at ease. And *then*, of course, we could talk turkey. I'd mostly listen at first, but I was always trying to figure out how and when to appropriately ask questions and participate. My goal was to be a nonthreatening part of the conversation.

I've always felt very strongly about women speaking up and speaking out and being noticed. And being proud to be women. There was a trend in the early '80s when women were wearing suits and ties and handkerchiefs to look just like men. I just couldn't understand that. I've never even owned a pantsuit! The last thing you want to do is blend in.

In the South, women always dress to look attractive. Looking attractive and being attractive is definitely part of the culture I was raised in. I had no problem being a woman playing sports, socializing, dancing, and having fun.

So when I came north, and got around some of the people who were high up in the women's movement, I was just surprised. I'm not entirely sure why they did it, but I think they felt like they had to dress like men to be accepted by men. The movement was so new and they were making it up as they went along, and they definitely had a tough fight gaining the attention, trust, and respect of the men in charge at the time.

I saw my femininity as who I am, and why should I downplay that? I didn't see anything wrong with standing out and being noticed. I wasn't about to change myself to accommodate men, or anyone else for that matter. That's critically important to me, to my identity. I've never changed myself to make someone else feel more comfortable, and I don't think other women should feel obligated to do that either. You need to be proud of who you are, whatever that may be! Find your own strengths and power and let those shine out. Be real and be you. People respect that; it's all about your self-esteem. And I love to see how people are embracing that today.

I know it's easier said than done because I feel like women still get so intimidated. Even the most successful women today get intimidated by powerful men; it drives me up a wall. Instinctively, the more powerful somebody is, the more aggressive I seem to be. Which gets me into trouble sometimes.

Aileen: And I get that … but I also know it's not an approach that works for every leader. It's perfect for you, Judee, because it's exactly who you are. Your personality and Southern roots mean leveraging your charm comes so naturally to you. I'm much more likely to lean on my expertise or gravitas to gain respect. And if I'm meeting someone powerful for the first time, I'd want to listen and observe for a while before making any bold moves.

Judee: Well, that still lines up with what I'm saying though. You have to be *you*. Show your true colors, whatever those colors might be. You're naturally more reserved than I am, and you're leading in a way that makes sense for you.

Aileen: Good point. I'm more than willing to experiment and explore as a leader, but I want to do my homework first! You love to make fun of me for being so buttoned-up, but a serious work ethic and dedication to learning are things I have always strived for. Willingness to learn has been helpful in my career in executive search, and a big part of my identity ever since I was a little girl.

Judee: I see that in you, for sure. Alongside your need to focus your work on a larger cause.

Aileen: Definitely. We both believe that the actions leaders take should ladder up to a worthy cause, to the service of something larger than themselves. Even when that path becomes incredibly challenging.

Judee: Well, let's keep going and dig into some of those challenges. And how we navigated them.

Chapter 2

Embracing the Challenges

In addition to being a soldier, a national security advisor, and now a CEO, I'm a mom to twin girls. In the previous chapter, I told you I strive to bring calm to chaos, but truthfully, it's not easy to subdue the chaos of parenting twins.

Shortly after my daughters were born, I found myself marveling at how exhausted I felt. Friends and family tried to warn me, but the reality was just too enormous to be described; it had to be felt. And I *felt* it.

Along with the overwhelm and sleep deprivation, I felt intense joy and fulfillment. Deep contentment, unlike anything else I'd ever known. Then, as my girls began to grow and interact with me more and more, over the coming months I noticed them watching me, observing me, sometimes mimicking things they'd seen me do or say. I wasn't just a mom to them; I was a role model. Which added more pressure, but also helped me do some valuable self-analysis. I wanted to show them humility, competence, flexibility … all of the traits I aspire to live by. And to do that, I had to get more comfortable in my own skin, own my strengths, avoid my personal pitfalls. I needed to balance my capabilities and challenges so I could be confident in the me they were studying so closely.

Basically, I realized that as you come up the ranks—whether that's in parenting or in your chosen profession—other people are internalizing the image of yourself you're projecting. If you don't calibrate that image to align with your genuine self, that dissonance can come back to bite you.

And bite me it did, though in an extremely constructive way.

So here's the story. I was part of an advisory board for a training program called WeLead, at American University's School of Public Affairs. The board was made up of mid-career professional women who had volunteered their time with postgrad women who wanted to work in policy or politics. Not long after the girls' first birthday, there was a Saturday session for WeLead where the board members were asked to sit on a series of panel discussions, talk about our experiences as leaders, and offer advice to the cohort. Sleep-deprived and ready for some weekend downtime, it took every ounce of my strength to leave my home on Capitol Hill and head over to the university to take part in this all-day session. But I was determined.

As I was getting ready for a panel, I heard one of the moderators reading out my bio to all these young women. When she was done, she said, "And she's a mom of twins, too."

I felt caught off guard. It was uncomfortable enough to hear someone rattling off my biggest accomplishments, making me sound like a big deal, but then to add "mom of twins" at the end made me sound like some sort of hero. The projected image of me didn't align with the real me, and that dissonance made me squirm.

I can't truly explain why I did this, but I decided to nip that in the bud, then and there. I saw all these women looking at me expectantly—busily creating a false image of me that they would file away under "invincible superwoman"—and I had to get vulnerable and real with them.

I said, "OK, that bio made me sound like I've got it all figured out, but here's the truth: I could barely get out of the house this morning. I cried three times on my way here. I'm barely keeping it together, and I want you all to know that. But I'm here."

It turned into a wonderful moment that opened up a conversation among all of the panelists and audience members. Everyone began to chime in about their own challenges in balancing their lives: work, school, dating, motherhood, aging parents, health. Many of us felt that, as women, we were struggling to create space for ourselves in our own lives.

Then we all shifted to the subject of comparison, how all young people—but young women in particular—hold themselves up to those they admire, which often makes them feel like failures. I've done it myself. I've also been so relieved when my heroes and mentors have chosen to be honest about their own struggles and challenges. Leaders who show their human side—who admit they aren't good at absolutely everything and ask for help when they need it—don't just win the trust of their teams and people. They remind aspiring leaders that power isn't about crafting a perfect track record that's utterly free of mistakes; it's about knowing how to stumble as gracefully as possible when things go wrong, and recover quickly. Resilience trumps perfectionism every time.

Judee: We both go to great lengths for our people, especially our families. It reminds me of the time I chartered a helicopter to make it to my son's elementary school graduation.

Aileen: What!? You've never shared that story with me.

Judee: I know, because it was such an over-the-top moment! I was scheduled to speak about women in leadership at a Penn State Women's Conference in Valley Forge, Pennsylvania, at 9:00 a.m. Ironically, I ended up discussing the lengths women go to, to balance work and family life. I pointed to the helicopter parked nearby and said, "Look at that helicopter. I've never been in one before, but I spent a thousand dollars to charter it so I wouldn't miss my ten-year-old boy's graduation this morning!" I recognized that this was extreme for me and that I was fortunate to have the means with which to pull off this stunt; nevertheless, the crowd cheered and clapped as I made my way to the helicopter. It took just fifteen minutes to get to my son's school, and I made sure the pilot parked far away so no one would see me arriving in a helicopter. I ran as fast as I could and made it just in time to wave and throw him a kiss as he walked to the stage. Family means the world to me, and I know it does to you too, Aileen.

Aileen: It does. And so does being transparent about the importance of my family. It isn't always easy to do, but whenever I think about holding back, I hear Brené Brown in my head reminding me about the power of vulnerability.

Embracing the Challenges   47

Judee: Being vulnerable as a leader can feel so risky, but it also shows strength in a funny way.

Aileen: Absolutely. And so does honoring someone else's vulnerability. Do you remember the first time we met, how I'd just had a skin cancer biopsy?

Judee: Oh yeah. On your forehead, right?

Aileen: Yes! I had an adhesive bandage in the middle of my forehead the day I was interviewing with you, and I was so self-conscious about it. I felt exposed and super vulnerable. And I remember right as you opened the door to greet me, I went to point to it and you said, "It's beautiful." And I just instantly relaxed. You saw the worry all over my face and swooped in to put me at ease.

Judee: Well, I wasn't about to let a little thing like that trip us up. We had work to do!

Aileen: We did. But I'll always remember that moment and how it made me feel. You used your power position to help me out, and I trusted you right away because of it.

Judee: That's a win for me, then.

Aileen: For both of us. Anyway, now that we're neck-deep in vulnerabilities and challenges and setbacks, do you want to dig into your law school story?

Judee: Might as well! As I said in the previous chapter, school was always a stumbling block for me, but that didn't keep me away.

If I'm being honest—and I usually am—I didn't do very well in school. Yet I insisted on going to college in an era when that was not *at all* expected of women.

So my parents were dumbfounded when I announced my decision. They just figured I would go to New York City to the Katherine Gibbs Secretarial School for executive secretaries, but I had exactly zero interest in doing *that*. So I got myself into Saint Mary's Junior College in Raleigh, North Carolina, which allowed me to head back south. And oh, I had a blast during my years there. I mean, I struggled academically because I was having too much fun to study ... but I got through.

Then I transferred to the University of North Carolina at Chapel Hill, where I proceeded to flunk math twice and get a D in economics. But I managed to get an A in political science.

Aileen: OK, I've gotta ask: why did you pursue all that schooling if school felt pointless to you?

Judee: Well, like I said earlier, I have always been ambitious, always eager to be at the table. School seemed necessary to be credible.

Aileen: Makes sense. Higher education isn't the only benchmark for leadership potential today—many companies are shifting to hands-on experience, skills, and competencies—but it still carries weight.

Judee: Believe me, it felt like a much bigger deal back in the '60s and '70s. Especially for women who were trying to enter the corporate workforce. We had to do a lot of proving ourselves.

Aileen: I can imagine.

Judee: Unfortunately for me, I just do not take naturally to studying, or testing, but I love to read newspapers and nonfiction. I devour them both!

Moving to my time working in Senator Mondale's office: a few years into my tenure as his personal assistant, I was pondering my next steps and decided to try law school. And I *loved* it. Studying criminal procedure and civil litigation absolutely fascinated me. For the first time in my entire life, I enjoyed school.

I'd applied to American University College of Law in January, I'd taken the LSATs, and around March or April, the dean called me and said, "Miss Metcalfe, don't take this personally, but you simply don't have an aptitude for law." Metcalfe was my maiden name. "You scored in the lower 10 percent of the nation." I was already in the middle of the semester, taking night classes, so I could still work for Mondale during the day, and I appealed to the dean to let me finish it out. He let me, reluctantly. So when it came time for exams, I glommed on to the smartest guy in the class, and we studied morning, noon, and night. And when I took the exams, I got three As and a B! Which made it possible to continue the degree.

Of course, the next semester, I sunk back to my normal level and got three Cs and a D. Simultaneously, my work in the senator's office heated up and I asked for a leave of absence from law school, which they gave me. I figured I'd go back, but I never did.

I regret that. A little bit, anyway. I certainly didn't have the time to go back to school and get good grades and hold down my increasingly demanding job. But I sometimes wonder how my life would have been different if I'd gotten that law degree.

Anyway, I think the lesson for me was about biting off more than I could chew. Again, I was never the best student, but I do believe if I'd focused on law school—and law school alone—I could have done well. Trying to juggle law school, full-time work in Mondale's office, plus my own social life and personal obligations was a full plate. I had to make choices, and I never doubted my job with Senator Mondale was my first priority. I wasn't going to let anything jeopardize that. It made me realize how challenging it all really was. It would help me later in life find the balance, set priorities, and understand the importance of managing my time, which, at least in my mind, would allow me to have it all. The lesson here is also focus and the importance of time management regarding your priorities. I have always been laser-focused on my priorities, and I never let anything distract me.

Embracing the Challenges　　51

Aileen: I bet you would've made a formidable lawyer, Judee.

Judee: Oh, I don't know. I really was enthralled that year I got to study the law, but actual practice as a lawyer is a whole different ball game. You have to be more consensus-driven, it seems, which is sometimes hard for those of us who are control freaks!

Aileen: Well, selfishly, I'm glad you took a different path. It means I get to learn from you and be alongside you. I know I've told you this many times, but I'm so grateful that I get to absorb your perspective, whether it's been on the industry, the economy, on leadership itself, on growing and scaling, or just on how to pick yourself back up after you've tripped.

Judee: Now you're making me blush.

Aileen: Well, it's all true. I already loved our industry before I met you, but teaming up with you has reinforced that what we do impacts economies, industries, and, ultimately, people. And you know I advocate for a people-first approach in all things.

Judee: Yes, you do. And rightly so. We both know that business is all about people.

Aileen: And, of course, you need the right people in the right roles. But I've learned that sometimes business success isn't about putting different people into leadership positions; it's about helping current leaders see themselves more clearly.

The executive search work we do at DSG includes advising and recruiting leaders, but other things too. We pride ourselves in our belief that finding the right leaders for the right institutions can truly change the world. However, we also recognize that the world is changing, and just as leaders are adapting, we have had to adapt in how we're helping those leaders be successful.

That means we might help them in a multitude of ways. Our deep-rooted relationships and the diversified experience and expertise that our colleagues bring allow us to work with our clients as partners to meet challenges and drive their business success.

By deeply understanding the market and integrating ourselves into our clients' journeys, we transition from a search-only approach to a comprehensive, strategic partnership. This allows us to leverage data and provide solutions that help clients overcome obstacles and achieve their goals.

Our support manifests in various forms and with various tools, including streamlining operations, expanding networks, embedding equity into systems, conducting in-depth assessments, advising on succession planning, and staying ahead of market trends.

One such tool that Aileen values is the AAR, or after-action review, a practice the army has used since the 1970s. The AAR is designed to extract lessons from one activity and equip teams to apply those same lessons to future activities. And it can be applied to both good and bad outcomes.

Embracing the Challenges   53

The AAR has become popular in the business world over the past few decades and many Fortune 500 companies are big fans.[10] *Harvard Business Review* has helped bolster that popularity by writing about the practice multiple times and urging those who use it to push beyond just discussing wins and losses and into using this in-depth review process to launch activities that will help repeat or avoid those same results.

An AAR can take many forms and be run at various levels of complexity, but essentially it asks people to gather after the conclusion of a project or event and consider the following questions:

- What was our mission?
- What actually happened?
- Why was there a difference?
- What have we learned?
- What will we do about it?

Aileen has worked with some of our clients to conduct these sessions at the end of a project or a search, and we also use them with our own teams internally. She believes that AARs can promote reflection and self-awareness that's helpful when things go right, but absolutely crucial when things go wrong. The process promotes continuous learning and humility, productive change, and accountability. And perhaps most importantly, resilience: the ability to recover from a challenging situation and get back on track.

In their brilliant book *The Prepared Leader*, Erika H. James and Lynn Perry Wooten write, "We do not ordinarily plan for the

---

[10] https://hbr.org/2023/01/a-better-approach-to-after-action-reviews

atypical, the anomalous, the irregular, or the exceptional on a day-to-day basis. We are hardwired to neglect the possibility of a crisis."[11] They go on to say that the best possible way to remain resilient through challenges and changes is to make preparedness part of a leadership team's embedded skill set. Just as James and Wooten advise, we counsel leaders and our clients to understand, manage, learn, and lead through all phases of a crisis instead of focusing solely on damage control.

All organizations face challenges and hit rough patches. We love it when we can help them find ways to understand, analyze, and learn from those difficulties so they can adapt quickly and come back stronger than ever.

Judee: Nobody enjoys analyzing their mistakes or getting negative feedback, but boy, if you don't do it, you just end up making the same mistakes over and over again.

Aileen: So true. The AAR is great for that. It can be a tough process, but it keeps people honest and helps them pinpoint areas of opportunity.

Judee: It can be tough being the truth-teller, too! We often are the ones who walk with our clients through those self-examinations and help them see the issues they've been avoiding. But I'm a big

---

[11] Erika H. James and Lynn Perry Wooten, *The Prepared Leader: Emerge from Any Crisis More Resilient Than Before* (Philadelphia: Wharton School Press, 2022), 6.

Embracing the Challenges 55

believer in the "no pain, no gain" philosophy. For myself, for companies, for everyone, really.

Aileen: I might soften that a little bit and say, "every failure contains a lesson and creates an opportunity." But I know what you mean.

Judee: I've certainly learned from my own missteps. And also from the risks I've taken over the years. Some of which panned out beautifully, and others … not as much.

Aileen: Risks are fantastic teachers, all right. Let's dive into those in the next chapter.

Chapter 3

The Confidence to Take Risks

I've given you a little peek at my time in Mondale's office over the past few chapters, but now it's time for the whole story.

When Hubert Humphrey was tapped from his seat in the US Senate to be Lyndon B. Johnson's vice president in 1965, Walter Mondale was appointed to fill out his term. Mondale arrived in DC as an ambitious, driven, whip-smart rookie senator who very much needed to fill out his support staff. And do so with people who had Minnesota addresses.

Now, I had made my way out of the Department of Commerce's secretarial pool and was working for a government contractor called Aerojet General when I heard about all this. And as it happens, I could claim a Minnesota address: my dad had become a top executive at 3M, which was headquartered outside Saint Paul, so my parents had relocated there. Not only that, but my dad also knew Joe Karth, the congressman who was helping Mondale get his new staff hired! So he introduced me, and I interviewed, and I was lucky enough to make the cut. But the folks who were already hired heard my Southern drawl and told me, "You can be one of the secretaries, but you can't answer the phone because you don't sound like you're from Minnesota. We're up for reelection, and it would confuse our constituents to hear your accent over the phone when they call." I said I could just tell callers I was from South Saint Paul—which I thought was pretty clever—but they weren't having it. So I stuck to non-phone tasks initially.

The senator already had a personal secretary, and through a series of events, she left and it was suggested that I replace her. Which I thought was a fabulous idea except for one problem: I didn't know how to take shorthand.

For you readers who grew up in the digital age, shorthand was a method of writing down a whole bunch of information very quickly by using abbreviations and symbols. It was mostly used for taking dictation, and I'd never learned it. But it was common practice back then for bosses to dictate to their secretaries.

Talk about a professional risk.

Luckily for me, Mondale's administrative assistant, Mike Berman, knew I was up a creek and offered to help me out. He said, "You just go in there and let him dictate. I'll be outside the door, listening and taking it all down in shorthand."

So the first time we tried out this arrangement, I went in with my pad, and Mondale started dictating. Mostly short letters, thank you notes. Stuff like, "Dear Lyndon, Great to see you last night. I look forward to working with you." They were simple, but he talked fast and dictated about thirty letters to me in one sitting. I was sitting there, just scribbling away, sweating buckets. When he was all done, he looked up and said, "Gosh, this is great. Call Joan

The Confidence to Take Risks   59

and tell her I'm on my way home." (He always used to have me call his wife to let her know that he was leaving the office. I thought that was kind of sweet.)

Anyway, he left and I went out to my little red Selectric typewriter, and Mike Berman walked in and read everything he'd captured in shorthand by listening through the door! I typed it all up on Mondale's personal stationery. We had a whole stack of letters, clean and error-free, and ready to go. The next morning, Mondale came in and was so pleased that the letters were all done.

Of course, Mike and I knew this wouldn't work forever.

Mike said, "Senator, why don't we get you a Dictaphone? Judee should really spend her time doing the scheduling and coordinating your committee hearings. With a Dictaphone, you can just dictate whenever it's convenient, and then she'll transcribe it all for you later."

So that's what we did. I was Mondale's personal secretary for the next ten years, and never did learn to take dictation. I assumed he had no idea, but the day I left, at my farewell party, I found out he'd known all along. He recounted that first session with a big smile!

You've probably heard about the study that found men will apply for a job when they meet only 60 percent of the qualifications, but women apply only if they meet 100 percent.[12] Clearly, I don't subscribe to all that. In my case, I knew I had to really dig deep to meet the demands. Mike Berman worked with me and taught me the ropes. I worked 24/7 and was available and on call to handle any problems and to avoid mistakes.

---

[12] https://hbr.org/2014/08/
why-women-dont-apply-for-jobs-unless-theyre-100-qualified

That job changed my life in so many positive ways. So clearly, that risk paid off.

Judee was just twenty-three when she took that job in Mondale's office. She was young and full of confidence. Many people think that taking risks is much easier when you're young, and perhaps it is. But both of us have continued to take both professional and personal risks throughout our lives. We've done so in different ways and different contexts, but we both believe that embracing some measure of risk is crucial in effective leaders.

We've also both watched gifted leaders of all ages and across various sectors navigate the world of risk with insight and acumen. Ralph Roberts, a Philadelphia icon, is a great example and one who was known for taking some big chances over the course of his career. A born entrepreneur and master marketer, he dabbled in everything from manufacturing golf clubs to running the advertising department at Muzak. But when he transitioned to venture capitalism and someone approached him to buy a small cable TV station in Mississippi in 1963, he hesitated. Roberts knew nothing about this emerging business, and it was wildly different from anything he'd done before. But in the end, he went for it, mitigating some of the risk by insisting that the station handle its own financial obligations. Soon after, he began buying up more cable stations under the same terms, and by 1969, he'd launched a little endeavor you may have heard of: Comcast.

Naturally, Roberts learned a ton about running media companies over the course of his thirty-three years of leadership at Comcast. But that initial leap was a big one. It could've backfired in a dozen spectacular ways. He trusted that partnering with experts and growing the business strategically would lead him to success. And he was right: Comcast became one of the largest global media and technology companies in the world.[13] That happened right here in Philadelphia, and he was one of my earliest clients back in the early 1980s. What an amazing role model he became.

In the business world, it's easy to associate risk with recklessness or negligence. And some emerging leaders believe that risk avoidance will create a solid career foundation, especially if they work in a new or disruptive industry. But as organizational psychologist Adam Grant has said, "Building a career isn't about avoiding risk. It's about managing risk. Think of your career like a stock portfolio: higher returns involve more risk. If all your bets are safe, it may be time to rebalance. In the long run, our biggest regrets are often the risks we didn't take."[14]

And we couldn't agree more. Risk can feel tenuous, but without it, there's no growth or learning. And a stagnant leader is an ineffective leader. To remain agile, attuned, and adaptable, leaders must become comfortable with risk-taking.

Of course, an "all risk, all the time" philosophy can be just as catastrophic as a zero-risk one. Part of growing into a leadership role is understanding risk and the necessary balance.

---

[13] https://www.investors.com/news/management/leaders-and-success/ralph-roberts-comcast-founder-biography/

[14] https://twitter.com/AdamMGrant/status/1445728741133537280?lang=en

Aileen: I definitely feel like preparedness and nimbleness are key to navigating uncertainty and handling risk. Some of that I learned from my military training, but it also comes from observing businesses flounder when they haven't trained to expect the unexpected. General Stanley McChrystal said, "If you strengthen your risk immune system, when the unexpected happens … you're going to be more resilient."[15] I'm with him on that. Curious to know your thoughts on risk preparedness, Judee.

Judee: I agree. However, I often like to shoot from the hip as I go with my instincts and enjoy the risk. But when it comes to things that seriously impact our people and our business, I'm more cautious. I also think you can overdo preparedness and end up in analysis paralysis!

Aileen: I'm definitely the more cautious of the two of us. Though I can't see either of us flying by the seats of our pants in a client meeting or press interview.

Judee: True. Though I've occasionally exaggerated to make a point and to get people to focus and pay attention. A minor risk, in my mind.

Aileen: I feel like you also hire seasoned experts into DSG as a way to mitigate risk for the company.

---

[15] https://bigthink.com/thinking/risk/

Childhood

Judee has always stayed active, whether as a little girl riding her bike or a teen swinging a golf club.

Aileen learned the value of teamwork and challenging herself through sports. Whether stopping a goal as the goalkeeper or supporting from the sidelines, she always understood the importance of playing her part for the team.

Aileen played baseball with the boys—and didn't need to hit off a tee to do it.

Aileen with her Nana at a special occasion.

Family

Aileen with her husband, Greg, on their wedding day.

Judee and her husband, Clay, at The William Penn Awards reception.

Judee with her family during the holiday season.

Judee taking a photo of her grandchildren and her daughter-in-law, Shannon. (Look in the mirror for the photographer.)

Early career

Executive assistant Judee with her boss, Senator Walter Mondale. He wrote on the signed photo, "To Judee, with eternal gratitude for your magnificent, gifted and loyal help. What on earth am I going to do now? With every good wish."

Judee (in glasses) looking over paperwork at Distaffers, the company she would later buy and transform into Diversified Search Group.

Aileen as a 2nd Lieutenant with her parents, Aileen and Frank.

Aileen with Greg and their two daughters on a trip to Colorado.

Aileen found the US Army to be a place for teamwork and camaraderie.

Executives, connected

Judee has long been involved and influential in Democratic Party politics. Here she is (counterclockwise, from upper left) with President Barack Obama; Hillary Clinton; in between the leader of the Special Olympics International Board of Directors Tim Shriver (left) and then-DSG CEO and President Dale E. Jones (right); and with Valerie Biden (center) and "Morning Joe" co-host Mika Brzezinski (right).

Aileen at The Catalyst Awards with Mike Hyter, to whom she previously reported.

Aileen speaking at the U.S. Chamber Talent Forward conference.

Aileen speaking at our firm's conference, "Navigating AI and New Tech for a Diverse and Responsible Tomorrow," with Myrna Soto in Ojai, California, (top) then taking a photo with some colleagues.

Aileen addressing participants at the 2023 Life Science Intelligence Emerging Medtech Summit.

Accolades, a lifetime of service

Giving back is a hallmark of Judee's career, and she has been recognized by many organizations for her service, including at the Globy Awards (top) and winning the William Penn Award (bottom).

Judee speaking to the Philadelphia Chamber of Commerce (top) and promoting civic engagement (bottom).

Judee delivering the keynote address at the DSG Managing Directors annual gathering in Philadelphia, 2022.

Aileen and Judee, though very different, have worked in tandem to great success for years. Here they are together at the Association of Executive Search and Leadership Consultants Conference (lower left), celebrating one of Judee's Lifetime Achievement Awards from the organization in 2022 (lower right), and proudly leading the DSG team at its 2022 conference in Philadelphia (top).

Judee—and DSG—always looking ahead.

The Confidence to Take Risks 63

Judee: I do know that I don't know everything, and a good leader builds teams full of people who fill in their own expertise gaps. But I am not afraid to take risks in hiring. Hiring you was a bit of a risk, Aileen! You'd never been a CEO before, but you had the character and tested background in multiple environments that aligned to our growth and complexity. My gut told me you were no dummy, you could relate to the future, and you had the right blend of preparedness and caution, along with the necessity of risk-taking.

Aileen: Accepting this CEO position was one of my biggest risks to myself, too. Second only to making the jump from policy work to the private sector.

I think of my career as having three main stages: Stage 1 is the army, Stage 2 is my time at the Pentagon and Capitol Hill working in policymaking, and Stage 3 is my work in the private sector.

I've told you some pieces of Stage 1 already, but now I'm going to talk about the transition from the realms of military and government into the private sector. It was a massive change for me. And it was a pretty risky one to boot, with a steep learning curve.

While working on Capitol Hill in 2009, I was part of a team drafting the National Defense Authorization Act in the House of Representatives. Pregnant with twins, I was determined to see the bill through to prove that a mom could handle such important work. But with my husband and I both juggling careers, and with babies on the way, I began to contemplate my next career move. I started thinking about a move to the private sector, which I knew virtually nothing about. It was a decision fraught with risk.

But several leaders I admired had begun to champion the "tri-sector athlete" approach to leadership, which was eventually codified by political science scholar and policy expert Joseph Nye. He describes a tri-sector leader as someone who can "engage and collaborate across the private, public, and social sectors."[16] Nye and others maintained that people who had this breadth of experience could more easily navigate various cultures, get teams aligned, and tackle sprawling problems.[17] All of that appealed to me, big time. I loved the idea of deliberately cultivating experience sets from different sectors that could help me lead in an increasingly complex, interconnected, and dynamic world.

The next logical step for me felt like the private sector, but I wasn't sure where to find my entry point.

Luckily one of my professors from Harvard's Kennedy School, where I'd earned a master's in public policy, had continued advising me long after graduation, so I asked if I could pick his brain. His name was Dr. John White, and he'd had a deeply impressive career. He was a lieutenant in the United States Marine Corps, served as chairman and CEO of Interactive Systems Corporation before the company was bought out by Kodak, taught at Harvard, and served as deputy secretary of defense during the Clinton administration. He has since passed away, but was a valued mentor to me for many years, especially during transitions in my career.

---

[16] https://hbr.org/2013/09/triple-strength-leadership

[17] https://hbr.org/2013/02/why-the-world-needs-tri-sector

Dr. White knew me well and I trusted him, so as we chatted on the phone, I asked him point-blank what he thought I should try next. It was still somewhat early in my career, but I was also a new mom and not sure what might be a good fit for someone like me. He had me do a reflective exercise about my personal and professional skills and experiences. He put me in touch with a colleague of his who was a partner at one of the top executive search firms in the country. Like Dr. White himself, this man had worked in business, served in the military, and done policy work. He was a tri-sector athlete who could weigh in about this approach to leadership and hopefully offer me some guidance.

He was incredibly generous in listening and offering me advice. As I described my own experiences and passions, he smiled.

"It sounds like you have a real passion for leadership, empowering people, and building teams," he told me. "Do you know what I do?"

I said, rather sheepishly, "I have no idea."

As he described executive search to me—a field that advised companies on their leadership needs and positioned them to attract and identify leaders who could help them achieve their top priorities—it sounded fantastic. Especially since I hadn't spent any time in the private sector yet, and this work would give me a chance to observe and learn about a whole slew of industries. And do it while I was advising companies on leadership roles.

On top of all that, by this time my twin daughters were ten months old, so I was hoping to move into a line of work that required less travel and fewer hours. My work with the House Armed Services Committee alone took me to Europe, the Middle East, Asia, and Latin America on congressional delegation trips; I was incredibly grateful for those experiences, but also ready to be home with my family more often. Capitol Hill isn't exactly known as a place that keeps normal office hours, and I was craving more flexibility. So I thought, *I'll do this for a couple years and catch my breath. I'll learn more about what's out there, get some experience in industry, and build out my network.*

I was excited, but also knew that pitching my own work-life experience to suit this new-to-me industry would be a challenge! I'd been a captain in the army, then worked in international security and defense policy for the Department of Defense and US Congress. How could I express what I'd done in those roles in a way that would appeal to executive search firms? Did I actually have the experience needed to make this leap into the private sector? Was this too risky of a pivot for me to take?

I decided it was just risky enough, *and* a phenomenal learning opportunity.

I saw that much of my policy work was about advising and consulting and connecting the dots—high-level thinking and maneuvering that would translate seamlessly into advising business leaders on their strategic priorities. In my previous roles, I'd learned to say "yes" if I saw a chance to develop myself as a leader or as a person, and was always ready to take on jobs that people around me thought I shouldn't. I loved learning and taking roads less traveled. Dating back to my childhood, moving to a new state every few years, I'd cultivated comfortability with change and a fascination with trying new things. And, of course, my ever-present drive to be of service would be useful in executive search. A career where I'd be able to help both companies and individuals be more successful—where I'd be supporting leaders in making their industries better—sounded exciting and fulfilling.

The Confidence to Take Risks 67

So as I began interviewing, I focused on what Dr. White had pointed out to me: that I was drawn to anything related to leadership and loved encouraging other people. I added that my time in DC allowed me to observe different leaders and decision-makers, political appointees, and general officers at some of the highest levels of our government; I'd made a study of different leadership styles and perspectives and was eager to apply that knowledge. And my experience in the army gave me insight into states of readiness. In a military context, we talked in terms of training readiness, but I could apply that knowledge to board readiness or C-suite readiness, too. I learned to recognize individuals who valued preparation and showed adaptability and resilience. Those were the people ready to advance and do big things.

I guess I made my case well, because I ended up working for two of the largest firms in the industry. Throughout those early years, I felt like I was getting paid to get an MBA. I worked with and learned from some incredible colleagues, some of whom had been executives from industry, others who had risen through the ranks in executive search and consulting, and even a former Navy SEAL. I was also fortunate enough to meet and work with leaders and CEOs in dozens of different sectors. One day I might be working with a Fortune 100 company, the next a growth-stage private-equity-backed company, and the next a nonprofit. As it turned out, the hours in executive search were just as long—if not longer—than those of a policy advisor. But I had the autonomy and flexibility I wanted, the ability to be with my family when they needed me, even a hybrid work schedule before that became the norm. The pivot paid off.

And after a few years, another pivot presented itself. While the transition from policy to executive search was a risky one, so was my decision to move from my old firm to DSG.

It was the middle of the pandemic and I had every intention of staying put; I was at one of the largest executive search firms in the world and was on track to build a solid career for myself. I was the sole breadwinner in my family at the time. COVID-19 had turned the world on its head, and maintaining stability seemed more important than ever. My income mattered to my family, and I wasn't looking to rock the boat.

But then George Floyd was murdered, and the events that followed forced me to take a closer look at how I could contribute to something bigger than myself, support those who needed it most, make a real and lasting difference. I've always felt a call to service, and in that volatile time, I realized I wanted my professional life to have more of an impact. Like anyone who serves in the armed forces, that urge never leaves you.

And just as I was beginning to mull over how I might make this happen, I got a call about the potential for succession to CEO at DSG.

I was floored and honored, and even though I wasn't looking for a change of that magnitude, it all seemed pretty fateful! Judee was an icon in the industry. She had made a name for the firm as one that was genuinely dedicated to filling executive roles by looking more widely at what it takes to be a great leader, and she herself was philanthropically and civically engaged in the local Philadelphia community. That struck a real chord with me. Especially given what was happening in the world.

I got on a call with Judee as a first step. I remember I was sitting in my home office and thought, *This will be a fifteen-minute call, tops.* Then we talked for an hour and a half. We just kept finding

The Confidence to Take Risks 69

more connection points, both professional and personal. I was amazed.

Then I agreed to meet with her for dinner.

Judee: I've got to jump in here and say a few things. First of all, the dinner was at my house, on a gorgeous summer night, and it was the same night Aileen was so worried about that little blemish on her forehead. (That was back in Chapter 2, in case you missed it.) We had a fantastic time getting to know each other. I always say we got her at a weak moment. She was well positioned at her last firm, and she wasn't looking for a change, but I think she was curious about what coming over to DSG might be like.

Aileen: I was curious, definitely. Also in a really contemplative phase and trying to figure out how to do work that encompassed all aspects of myself.

Judee: We just clicked that night. I knew right away that Aileen was the right one.

Aileen: And I always claim that my main advantage was that I was at the beginning of the alphabet, being Aileen Alexander when it came to interviewing.

Judee: We're going to have this fight forever, aren't we?

Aileen: Yeah, probably.

Judee: Well, if you want the truth, it had nothing to do with alphabetical order and everything to do with who Aileen is as a person. She was—still is—a woman of great character and integrity. Just over a single dinner, it became so obvious that she has the values we really treasure at DSG. We have always felt that we have a pretty unique culture, and we needed someone who would add to that culture and bring our shared values across the platform as we grew. And, of course, Aileen is from a younger generation and could help us transition toward the future.

Aileen: But as you said earlier, hiring me was a risk. So … we were taking risks on each other, simultaneously.

Judee: I guess so!

Aileen: You know, when I left your house after dinner that night, I pulled out of your driveway and parked just past the first stop sign I saw. I called my husband and he said, "How did it go?" and I said, "I think our whole life is about to change."

Judee: Did you really?

Aileen: True story.

Judee: Oh, I just love that.

The Confidence to Take Risks   71

Aileen: And after the transition period and coming on board officially, you've been there with me, guiding and advising. You've been a real thought partner to me, giving me such good counsel as I've learned the ropes. Though you've also known when to let me make my own mistakes, to trip and stumble and scab my knee—because that's how I'm going to learn.

Judee: I try to, and will always have your back.

Aileen: Oh, I know. And we've never said that you're mentoring me; you're Mondale-ing me. Sometimes you'll slip into my office to see if I need a Mondale moment, and even if I don't, I usually take the opportunity to get you talking and absorb some wisdom.

Judee: Now you're just flattering me.

Aileen: I'm not, and you know it. When I'm faced with big decisions, I've usually got 87 percent of what I need with the help of our talented DSG executive leadership team, but the other 13 percent comes right from you. I either ask you or channel you; either way, it's your wisdom that gets me over the finish line. But hey, let's switch gears a little now and talk about other risks you've taken with DSG. Anything specific come to mind?

Judee: Actually, yes. And it's another hiring decision.

In the late '70s, I hired a guy to join the very small DSG team. He was a professor at Wharton and one of the smartest people I've ever known. A friend introduced us, and I could tell right away that he would fit in with us, so I hired him.

A week or so after he started, he came into my office and shut the door. Then he said, "There's something I have to talk to you about."

And I said, "All right. What is it?"

He said, "I'm gay."

And I said, "So? Who cares?"

Now, there had been some strides in LGBTQ+ rights in the '70s, but we still had a long way to go. The first federal gay rights bill was introduced to the US Congress in 1975 but never made it past the Judiciary Committee. Just a few years before, in 1973, the American Psychiatric Association had finally removed homosexuality from its list of mental disorders in the DSM-II (Diagnostic and Statistical Manual of Mental Disorders); before that, it was considered a mental illness to be gay![18] Plenty of workplaces would refuse to hire people because of their sexual orientation, but that didn't enter my thinking, honestly. I believed he would do great work at DSG.

It might have been a risk to hire him, but I didn't see it that way. A sort of secondary risk came when I suggested he tell the rest of the team. There were only five of us at the time, including him, but we have had a culture of transparency from the get-go. Being gay was a controversial issue at the time, as was working with a gay man, but if someone on my team was going to have a problem with it, we wanted to know right away.

---

[18] https://www.cnn.com/2015/06/19/us/lgbt-rights-milestones-fast-facts/index.html

The Confidence to Take Risks 73

And sure enough, our other male employee came to me feeling … unnerved. He was a big, macho, married guy. He asked me, "Does this mean if the new guy uses my phone, I could catch something from him?"

I just rolled my eyes.

But that was the mentality back then. Nearly everyone was still closeted, and people who were "out" risked open discrimination. Come 1982, Wisconsin became the first state to outlaw discrimination based on sexual orientation, but plenty of other laws stayed put.[19] Not to mention social norms.

I'm glad we didn't subscribe to that attitude, that we chose to build a Deliberately Different internal culture from the start. Our hire did wonderful search work, and he was a terrific employee. People really admired him, and he brought other incredibly helpful perspectives to evaluating candidates. I think it's important for leaders to be open to debate and discussion and different points of view. You don't want to be surrounded by people who all hold the same opinions. Echo chambers just lead to stagnation.

VUCA is an acronym that first appeared in US Army War College documentation in 1987 and has since been adopted by the business world. It stands for volatility, uncertainty, complexity, and ambiguity, four terms that perfectly describe the world we live in today.[20] Since technology, culture, and the entire business landscape

---

[19] https://www.cnn.com/2015/06/19/us/lgbt-rights-milestones-fast-facts/index.html

[20] https://usawc.libanswers.com/faq/84869

are all changing at breakneck speed, leaders who stagnate have become actual liabilities to their companies and teams.

And as Judee points out, teams full of people who bring varied perspectives to bear are a surefire way to keep leaders open to change.

Aileen's take on this strategy is to "lead through others." She's found that if everything rests with her alone, the dynamic shifts to command-and-control, which makes it impossible to keep pace with constant change. In a world that's constantly evolving, it's not just different perspectives and experiences that need to be elevated and heard; it's distributed leadership. More people need to feel ownership and be entrusted to lead in order for endeavors to move forward quickly.

Keeping communication open and flowing in all directions is another crucial way to avoid stagnation; great ideas can surface from anyone at any time, and great leaders must be receptive to them.

Every company or organization will need to choose its own ways to keep innovation alive. The point is to ensure that the global rate of change doesn't make you risk-averse. Risks should be gauged and considered carefully, but never avoided entirely. As president and COO of TIAG Neil Lampton wrote, "The act of leading involves guiding a team or organization through change with no guarantee of success, hoping to come out better on the other side. In short: Without risk, there's no need for leaders."[21]

Gauging risk can be tricky. It's often more of an art than a science. Aileen will follow her instincts, but is also apt to carefully

---

[21] https://www.forbes.com/sites/forbestechcouncil/2023/10/25/
the-dangers-of-playing-it-safe-six-truths-about-why-and-how-leaders-need-
to-take-risks/?sh=2de474d66c95

observe the players, gather as much background information as she can, and weigh the pros and cons. Judee relies on her gut when determining if a risk is worth taking, and with decades of experience under her belt, she has honed her ability to sniff out a good bet. But she will also jump into a risk, feet first, if the stakes are relatively low.

Judee: Do you remember when I was so moved by the newly elected Philadelphia mayor Cherelle Parker's speech that I had an instant urge to personally contribute significantly to her efforts?

Aileen: Do I ever …

Judee: Well, you know, I felt like it was incredibly important to support her. She had just given a rousing forty-five-minute speech at the 2024 Mayoral Luncheon to a crowd of about two thousand people, and they loved her. Cherelle is a great orator and had the crowd energized and caught up in her plans. She announced that Amazon had just agreed to donate $100,000 to Philadelphia Taking Care of Business (PHL TCB), her new neighborhood commercial corridor cleaning program, which was great, and everyone cheered. I thought to myself, I need to do something to support her. And once she got off the stage, I went up to her and said, "You are unbelievable. I'm so proud of you. I'm going to personally make a sizable contribution to you, and you and I are going to sit down and decide where we can put it to best use."

Aileen: That's you, Judee: generous and strategic.

Judee: Well, Mayor Parker is the 100th mayor and she is the first woman! We've got to support her. I've always felt giving back to the community was a top priority. And as I was listening to her speak, it just hit me: this is what I care about. She's the mayor of the sixth largest city in the country, and I'm going to do everything I can to help her.

Aileen: I bet you are. And you know, your values are one of the reasons I was drawn to work here in the first place. I knew you contributed significantly to the civic health and well-being of local communities. That aligns so well with my drive to serve.

Judee: I could see that so clearly from the first time I met you. Dinner at my house.

Aileen: I definitely don't make a secret of it.

Judee: True. But it wasn't just what you said. It was how you said it. Your tone and emphasis. Along with how you reacted to me describing the job, the company mission, our culture. I could see you were what the firm needed for leadership in the future, and you just happened to be a woman! Best of all!

Aileen: And that's where we're headed next, topic-wise: taking cues, understanding interpersonal signals, reading body language …

The Confidence to Take Risks 77

Judee: … all the best strategies for observing people and reading rooms.

Part 2

ESSENTIAL TRAITS FOR THE MODERN LEADER

Chapter 4

The Art of Reading the Room

My time in the army helped me build multiple skill sets that have proven incredibly valuable to me as a CEO, but the most valuable one might just be adaptability.

From contingency planning to after-action reviews (AARs), I spent years developing muscle around being coordinated, nimble, and flexible. Because nothing about combat is ever predictable, and you've got to train and be prepared to react quickly to a wide variety of scenarios. As General Stanley McChrystal has said of both business and military action, "Efficiency remains important, but the ability to adapt to complexity and continual change has become an imperative."[22]

Adaptability has helped me both read and react to many different environments. Here's one room-reading experience that made all the difference in my ability to perform and deliver.

---

[22] https://www.linkedin.com/posts/stanmcchrystal_efficiency-remains-important-but-the-ability-activity-6800778919554371584-osSf/

I'd been invited to keynote at the 2023 Life Science Intelligence (LSI) Emerging MedTech Summit, and had prepared a talk on three dimensions of leadership that reach beyond industry, rank, or position. I'd spent a lot of time on this keynote; I tend to write over the course of multiple iterations regardless of the topic, and since this felt like an opportunity to connect my military experience with my current position as CEO, I spent even more time than usual refining my remarks. I'd prepared a fifteen-minute talk and was excited to be one of the speakers kicking off the event by sharing my leadership philosophy with a crowd of nearly a thousand attendees.

Then the event staff opened the bars.

The waiting, murmuring crowd that was milling around the tented space suddenly began to break up and cluster around the various bartender stations, ordering and sipping their free drinks. In mere minutes, the talking got louder and the people got rowdier. Going up to my hotel room to get ready, I knew I needed to revise my plan, and fast. These people were not going to tolerate fifteen minutes of … well, anything. The situation had changed, and I needed to revise my plan and adapt to it.

With very little time, and adrenaline pumping, I had to pivot. So I sat down with my three-page speech, folded it in half, called a colleague, and handwrote a much shorter (and probably more interesting) version consisting of an opening and just three main points. Despite all the preparation, I had to "wing it" and deliver remarks that were both substantively and stylistically different. But it made all the difference.

Being able to read the room, keep calm, and shift my plan in the moment served me well. I delivered my truncated speech to a loud and rowdy crowd, but my message was well received overall and led to some great feedback, connections, and even new opportunities. If I'd stuck to my original plan and waded through my entire prepared remarks, I guarantee it would have been a total disaster.

And the real kicker? One of the three dimensions of leadership I spoke about that day was contingency planning. I kid you not. Little did they know that I was playing it out in real time!

In addition to *getting into* the rooms that matter, the ability to read a room—take the emotional temperature of attendees, identify power players, understand when to speak and when to listen—is a skill that all leaders, now more than ever, need to put to good use. It's a mixture of self-awareness, empathy, observation, and attunement to social cues that helps build trust and foster collaboration. A leader who aligns with and responds to the energy of a group has a far easier time getting support and alignment than one who plows ahead with their agenda regardless of the reactions they're getting.

This leadership skill is priceless across all possible use cases, as evidenced by this insight from the late, great Kobe Bryant:

> To be an effective leader, you have to be a really good listener and not to what's being said, but to what's *not* being said. You have to be really observant. That was a big transition for me. I went from being a scorer and a floor general … to being a leader and that meant putting others first. That means not worrying about are you in

rhythm, are you playing well in this game, are you ready to go, to [asking yourself] are they ready? What can I do to help them be ready?[23]

We think he's spot-on. Of course, it's much easier to determine how people are feeling when you are face-to-face in smaller groups than it is when you're delivering a keynote to a crowd from a stage in a darkened room (unless, of course, the event staff opens the bars before you even make it to the podium). But in either case, leaders need to find ways to read all sizes of rooms, in order to communicate effectively.

Tuning in to the attitudes of other people at events and meetings also helps us create a sense of inclusion. Aileen particularly enjoys being a disrupter of rooms where people have clustered together in their comfort-zone groups, whether the groups are by business department, leadership level, or social familiarity. In a previous role, she worked for a company that held popular monthly lunches, and Aileen would casually and gently walk around and challenge everybody to sit at different tables. She saw this as an opportunity to help people broaden their experience, promote understanding, and ultimately be more engaged and productive.

Both of us know that reading the room can also include curating your own table thoughtfully, inviting specific people to sit with you. The politics of seating is extremely significant, and leaders can leverage that by inviting new hires, people from different levels within the organization, more diverse groups, and others to join

---

[23] https://www.cnn.com/2020/01/27/us/quotes-kobe-bryant-trnd/index.html

The Art of Reading the Room 85

them. People want to feel included and appreciated, and this is a subtle yet powerful way for leaders to demonstrate that.

We both observed heads of state and national and state level officials who excelled at reading people and working the room. They knew just who to connect with, how to put them at ease, and how to welcome them into the fold. In fact, politicians and government officials—and leaders in most arenas—who have real longevity are often the ones who can walk into virtually any room, get a sense of undercurrents and sub-agendas, and make real connections with people. We found it interesting to watch them in action, and we learned a lot from them.

Aileen: When I was studying at the Harvard Kennedy School, and throughout those years I spent in Washington, DC, I got to interact with some world-class room-readers. From political appointees in the Bush and Obama administrations, to ambassadors and general officers, to members of Congress, the best ones paid attention to these details and were intentionally inclusive. They operated with a mix of gravitas and compassion. Judee, I'm sure you had similar experiences.

Judee: I had the honor of seeing John F. Kennedy speak several times, and no one could read a room and engage people, both one-on-one and in big crowds, like he could. He created an instant bond with people with his curiosity and inquisitiveness. Even in large groups, he'd always ask them questions. He also had a powerful delivery, with his Boston accent, and a strong voice that resonated and got attention. His use of humor was in a class by itself. No public figure I have encountered was better at it, except maybe his brother, Bobby Kennedy. John Kennedy exuded charisma wherever he went, and his inspiring words "ask not what your country can do for you—ask what you can do for your country," will live on forever. He was asking something of his audience, asking them to engage in these big efforts with him. That's why he was so inspiring. He created a meaningful connection with everyone he encountered.

Aileen: Honestly, I'm jealous.

Judee: The '60s were an incredible time in the history of our country. You saw what real leadership was all about. The good and the bad.

Aileen: I assume you witnessed politicians who really knew how to interpret body language and think on their feet. I saw it, too, at the Department of Defense and on Capitol Hill. I assume Mondale could hold his own in terms of reading rooms?

Judee: For sure! He was as smart as a whip, down-to-earth, personable, funny, and incredibly perceptive. Walter Mondale could read people as well as anyone I have ever known. He was amazing.

Aileen: Any other people from your own circle who are experts at reading the room?

The Art of Reading the Room   87

Judee: Have I told you about Helen Wilson?

Aileen: A little. But I think you should tell everyone about her. She was a huge influence on you, right?

Judee: Absolutely. And she helped me learn that misreading a room could turn into a disaster.

Helen Wilson was kind of my idol. She was twenty-one years older than I was and absolutely beloved by just about everyone in town. She was a legend in Philadelphia and one of the rare women at that time who was a true leader in the city. She was constantly receiving honors from all sorts of organizations, and she was a great speaker who knew how to use humor. Helen was incredibly accomplished—a nationally ranked golfer and owner of two of the most famous restaurants in the city—but she didn't take herself too seriously. She'd poke fun at herself, and tell these funny and engaging stories from her life. Her ego was totally intact, and her clear interest in others meant she was widely loved and admired.

She wasn't afraid to get a little out there, either, if the situation needed it. If she was attending a dinner or lecture and things were getting too serious or boring, she would put two spoons over her eyes and hold them there. It was subtle in some ways, but such a great, off-the-wall way to inject humor into a weighty room; it never offended anyone but got her message across. Time to lighten the mood!

I first met Helen when we were both serving on the board of Central Penn National Bank. I think I was thirty-nine, so Helen was around sixty. The bank executives in board meetings kept showing all these slides with figures and graphs and statistics. And I couldn't understand the numbers. (Remember how I flunked math twice in college?) So I kept raising my hand and asking questions about the slides. Lots of questions. Enough to really annoy the other board members, though I wasn't aware of that at the time.

After one of these meetings was over, the chair came up to me and said, "Judee, we need a sidebar."

I genuinely thought he was talking about furniture. So I said, "Well, where would you put it?"

He explained that he meant we needed to have a conversation, you know, off the record and away from everybody else. (That's two faux pas in one meeting, for those keeping score.)

Then he told me, "You've got to stop asking all these questions. It's disruptive. I'm happy to meet with you prior to the meeting and walk you through the numbers so you don't have to do that every time and prolong the meeting."

And I said, "OK, fine," and thanked him. I'd led meetings and given some speeches by that time in my career, but I'd never been on a public company board. I had no idea that board meetings had their own protocols and culture. I was grateful for the feedback, but also a little flustered.

Then Helen came up to me—she was already a member of the board—and she introduced herself. I sure knew who she was! And then she said to me, "Down, Fido."

Which was hilarious, of course, but also a bit of a friendly warning. She'd seen me clogging up these meetings with all of my questions, pretty much failing to read the room, and wanted to protect me. Get me to rein it in before I lose all credibility with the other board members.

After that, she was almost like a mother figure to me. Our families became very close, I invested in her restaurants, and eventually she came to work at DSG. She headed our sports and entertainment division for years, bringing in some world-class companies and leaders for us. Helen was a live wire, and everyone just adored her. I remember walking by a boardroom in our office one day, and the door was shut. I wondered what was going on in there. Come to find out she was giving the guys putting lessons!

Helen was the one who taught me the delicate art of reading and working rooms. I've always had a little bullshit in me, and that does *not* always serve me well in a serious boardroom environment. But it can also lighten things up sometimes. It's a fine line between that and going too far. In the boardroom, it becomes clear very quickly who the smartest people are—who's done their homework and who's adding value. Those are the people who will get everybody nodding and gradually position themselves to steer the whole conversation in whatever direction they've chosen. It's hard to bullshit in that environment, so you have to be careful. There's a right way and a wrong way to do it.

Helen and I were the only women on the board of Central Penn National Bank when we first met, and I loved seeing how she operated. She didn't have a college degree, but she was no slouch and worked hard to understand the complexities of matters being discussed. Her style was different from mine. She had arrived and proved herself as someone to be admired and respected, whereas I was living off having worked for the vice president of the United

States and had a long way to go to prove myself on my own. She was a great role model to me in terms of her character and integrity, in particular.

I'm so glad I got to know her and learn from her. Both her serious and her not-so-serious side. She showed me how to gauge when I could use humor, when I needed to focus on earning respect, and when I could push the envelope, depending on how the crowd was reacting. I'm forever grateful to her.

Aileen: I wish I could've met Helen.

Judee: Oh, me too. You two would've gotten on famously.

Aileen: The way you describe her, I can totally see how she influenced your ability to read rooms. Do you remember when you got the Globy Lifetime Achievement Award from the Global Philadelphia Association in 2022?

Judee: I sure do.

Aileen: I got to watch YOU pivot on a dime at that event. You were sitting next to me, editing your speech, and watching as honoree after honoree gave these long, formal speeches. The room was feeling a bit restless. At one point you leaned over and whispered to me, "I don't even know if I'm going to use this."

Judee: I remember that.

The Art of Reading the Room 91

Aileen: When you finally got called to the stage, you just folded up your notes and left them on the podium. You opened up your remarks with a joke that broke the tension instantly, like you often do. And even though all eyes were on you, you made that moment about everyone else in the room. Connected them to you and to each other. It was amazing to see you make that decision on the fly, and then make the absolute most of it.

Judee: Well, that's kind of you. I just didn't want to put anyone to sleep! And Aileen, you're no slouch when it comes to keeping an audience engaged, even when the gathering is virtual. I've seen you on our town hall meeting calls with three hundred people, all those faces on the screen. And you'll be talking about an idea or initiative, then say, " … and I'm looking at Susan, who's been doing this for ten years … " It's great. Helps people feel included and seen.

Aileen: Reading a virtual room is a skill I'm definitely still working to hone. But I like that tactic of mentioning people by name because it feels natural and calms my Zoom anxiety nerves, and it helps me make it super clear that I see us all as part of the same team, working toward the same goals. As we know, it's all about our people, and they deserve the credit.

Judee: I'm with you on that, as you know. Spread the credit, profit, and joy around. Always.

Aileen: I know we both also avoid talking too much about ourselves. Nothing kills the energy and engagement in a room like a leader who just keeps droning on, long after the other people have lost interest.

Judee: Especially when you're connecting with your own employees. They want to tell you about their lives, and they want to know that you care about them. They want you to remember that their daughter is in medical school or their spouse is a famous architect or whatever. If a leader just tells endless stories about their vacations or golf outings, they're going to lose the interest of their audience fast.

Aileen: And lose trust too, potentially. Reading rooms isn't just about adjusting your tone or changing your subject matter; it's about meeting listeners where they're at. Helping them participate by making them feel included.

Judee: And never be arrogant. Be human, be humble, poke fun at yourself, be confident—but never brag about what you've experienced or accomplished.

Aileen: I feel like humility is a core value for us both.

Judee: One hundred percent. Seeing leaders puffing themselves up in boardrooms or in front of crowds just makes me cringe.

Aileen: You know, I got some tough-but-honest feedback about my communication style a few years ago that wasn't exactly about bragging ... but definitely about being humble and connected as a leader.

Judee: Oh? I'd love to hear more about that.

I think of myself as someone who will observe and assess a room before I make my move. I try to see everything that's going on: body language, who's paying attention, where everyone has chosen to sit, who is dominating the conversation, who is wishing they could speak up but struggling to get their voice heard. I've been at the head of the table, I've been tucked in the back of the room, I've guided conversations, and I've fought to be heard. And I think when you're in a position of leadership, part of your responsibility is to read a room, and then create a sense of inclusion and belonging for everyone.

But several years ago, I found out I was doing something that was impacting my ability to connect and read a room.

A former boss of mine at my prior firm—Mike Hyter, who is now an expert in inclusive leadership and CEO of the Executive Leadership Council—gave me some constructive input around communications. I remember the conversation so clearly. We were both grabbing coffee in the company break room when he took me aside.

"Whether you're leading a room, at a table, or one-on-one, it's clear your mind is going a mile a minute," he told me. "You're thinking furiously and planning out your next move. I can see it on your face."

He was absolutely right, of course. When I'm in working mode, my brain is firing on all cylinders at all times.

"The problem is you're not listening. When your mind is racing and you're busy deciding what you're going to do or say next, you're not hearing what others are saying. And to be an effective communicator, you've got to be an effective listener."

Again, Mike was right. That advice wasn't fun to hear, but as soon as he offered it, I knew it was both true and important. And if I took it to heart, I would become exponentially better at reading rooms, connecting with people, advising clients, and being fully engaged as a leader.

So I focused on becoming an active listener, regardless of the situation. I cultivated better habits. Now, I remove distractions from my environment, silence my phone, practice eye contact. And I lean on strategies that are incredibly helpful at tuning in to the dynamics of groups of people: I pay attention to body language (especially signals that people are uncomfortable), I listen to tone of voice, I repeat back to people anything that felt even a little unclear, and most importantly, I don't plan out what I'm going to say while someone else is speaking.

I thanked Mike for this feedback; it truly changed me. His observation and comment reminded me that reading a room is actually grounded in listening. There are definitely visual elements, but if you try to gauge the attitude of a group of people just by looking at them, you'll miss out on tons of vital information. Listen to what they're telling you, what they're not telling you, and how they're choosing to say it.

When I started doing that more actively, every room felt more readable.

Reading rooms isn't a skill, it's a skill *set*. It involves picking up on context clues, noting reactions and interactions, understanding interpersonal dynamics, and responding to them in the moment. Some leaders can do all of these things instinctively; others need more practice. In an era when so many of our interactions are digitally mediated, it can be challenging to interpret body language or decipher context, so even leaders who've done well at reading in-person rooms may feel challenged now.

Both of us believe, though, that reading rooms is a necessary skill set for all modern leaders. Those who learn and practice it are more attuned, empathetic, and engaged, which in turn makes them more respected and trusted. Those who disregard the reactions of others, who bulldoze through groups without picking up on social cues, often end up alienating the very people they were hoping to win over.

Since reading rooms comes down to observing and understanding people, it's tied to emotional intelligence, or EQ. Dale Carnegie famously said, "When dealing with people, remember you are not dealing with creatures of logic, but with creatures of emotion," and he's perfectly right. Facts, statistics, and careful research should all reside in a leader's toolbox, but without EQ, it's tough to build lasting loyalty and meaningful relationships. And relationships are what leading is all about. Being human and authentic gets you everywhere!

In the next chapter, we'll talk more about how we've chosen to build and maintain such relationships with our peers, bosses, and employees by showing how much we care. Another element of EQ and another practice we both value deeply.

Chapter 5

It's All about Your People

You met my dear friend Helen Wilson in the previous chapter, and now I'm going to share a bit more about her. As I mentioned, we hired her to head DSG's sports and entertainment division, and she brought in a ton of valuable business. Everyone wanted to work with Helen, since her clients were golf celebrities like Arnold Palmer and Tom Fazio, as well as media and entertainment celebrities. And, of course, we all loved having her around the office. She made every meeting more fun, she could read people and situations better than anyone, and her humor and love of life were great for the culture.

Then, in the late '90s, she became very ill. Her doctor here in Philadelphia couldn't land on a diagnosis, so several of us took her to specialists in California and to Mayo Clinic in Minnesota to figure out what was going on. She was beloved and admired by all—and one of my closest friends—so I was determined to help her get the help she needed. Eventually Helen was diagnosed with a rare blood disease, one that wasn't treatable.

It took the wind right out of her sails, and for somebody who was used to being so active, that was tough. She ended up in a nursing home during the hardest part of her battle with the illness, and our team insisted on visiting her regularly. We'd bring her lunch or dinner, make her laugh, let her make us laugh. Everyone loved Helen, and everyone at our company treated each other like family, so getting a group together to go visit her and help lift her spirits was never a chore. People were eager to show her the same friendship, trust, love, and support she'd always shown them.

I remember when she started to fade. One morning, I went into her room and she was lying there, quiet and still. The hospital staff had said, "It's important to give people permission to die," and I took that to heart. So I held her hand and said, "It's OK, you can go. The window is open and you can go through." She didn't say a word, kept her eyes closed, was quiet as a mouse.

She didn't let go that day, so I came back the following morning. She was still asleep, so I started what the doctor said was good to say to her in terms of it being OK to go. Helen suddenly opened her eyes and said, "Are you going to do that whole 'open window' thing again?"

Down to her last breath, that woman had the best sense of humor.

When she died at age eighty-one, we had a big service to honor her, where there was a huge turnout. We printed up a lovely memorial booklet with photos and stories from her life; six people gave eulogies, including me; and the church was packed with friends and colleagues who would miss her vibrant presence. It felt like a true tribute to Helen, who had left such a great legacy behind her. At some point somebody came up to me and said, "I hope you're around when I die so you can put on an event like this for me." Nobody deserved it more than Helen, I thought. I wanted to celebrate my friend and send her off properly; that comment made me feel like we'd done her proud.

Everyone at DSG cared deeply for Helen, and she cared for them, too. She was a guiding force in many of our employees' careers, offering real wisdom and insight, but always kindly. She helped everyone learn not to take themselves too seriously. She lifted up the talented women leaders around her. Helen Wilson was a perfect example of how caring needs to be a two-way street between leaders and their teams.

***

Aileen: I still hear people in the office talking about how incredible Helen was. She definitely left a legacy that is ingrained in our culture.

Judee: Absolutely. She was one in a million. And she walked the talk, you know? She didn't just wax poetic about caring for her people and her teams; she actually lived it.

Aileen: Which is just critical, and rarer than it ought to be. I like to flip the army phrase, "Mission first, people always," to say, "People first, mission always." Looking out at a group of soldiers, it's so clear that's who you're leading, who you're taking care of ... and when you put their needs and development first, it's far easier to get aligned around a shared goal. Move toward the same horizon. I feel the same way now, looking out at our people.

Judee: So do I. It's honestly so strange to me that anyone would think a single leader could be responsible for a company's success. Every single person at our company is part of that, and I want them to know that we see their contributions. I know you do, too.

Aileen: Absolutely. And together we've tried some initiatives to make sure they all feel connected and cared for, especially since almost 75 percent of our people are dispersed. We do check-ins and virtual gatherings so we can make sure no one feels lost or out of touch. We travel to our various offices to break bread with our people and find out what's on their minds. I want the whole leadership team to be available to our people, as much as possible.

Judee: Showing you care, as a leader, is definitely different when everyone is spread across the country, and connecting only through their computers.

Aileen: Yeah, but you've found some great ways to do it over the years. Including truly generous profit-sharing. Did you tell me you gave away 40 percent of your ownership over the years, or made it available to others?

Judee: I did. I appreciate that running DSG is a huge, multi-person endeavor, and there's no way I could do it all myself! Also that our success isn't entirely my doing. So the way I see it, our people should benefit when the company does well. The leaders I admire most are the ones who share credit and success.

Aileen: It's such a great way to show your teams that you truly value their contributions.

Judee: Exactly. In my opinion, words only go so far. You've got to back up what you say with action. Prove it. Put your money where your mouth is, as literally as possible.

Verbal praise can be a wonderful way to show people you care about them, but most leaders of people know that deeds surpass words when it comes to memorable compassion. Both of us believe that finding concrete ways to champion and support people builds priceless trust and rapport, which are increasingly hard to come by in a world where leaders and their people may interact exclusively through smartphones and laptops.

Of course, we're far from the first to insist that leaders who care win the day. Dozens of studies have shown that happy employees lead to happy customers and better business results.

Recently, a group of researchers that included academics and industry experts investigated the importance of employee experience over three years and through one thousand organizations, then reported their findings to *Harvard Business Review*. They discovered that employees who felt stable, valued, and supported—through things like higher pay and deeper training—generated a 45 to 50 percent increase in profits per person per hour. And, at least in the case of this study, revenue increases were not accompanied by increased expenses.[24]

The two of us care deeply about leaders and leadership; our entire business is built on finding, developing, and convening individuals who can drive innovation, lead transformation, and shape the future of organizations. But we also know that leaders are nothing without the people who stand by them, brainstorm with them, tell them hard truths, keep their schedules in check, and help them execute on their visions. Gill Corkindale, executive coach and former management editor of the *Financial Times*, made this incisive observation:

> Senior executives like to show that they are important through their offices, dining suites and reserved car-parking places, but, in truth, their absence rarely affects the smooth running of a company. The same cannot be said about office administrators, facilities management staff, receptionists, canteen workers and cleaners. Without these people, companies soon start to fall apart—yet these are often the very people who are afforded the least recognition.[25]

The most effective leaders across various domains—including business, politics, education, social justice, and entertainment—

---

[24] https://hbr.org/2022/03/
research-how-employee-experience-impacts-your-bottom-line

[25] https://hbr.org/2007/12/put-people-first

understand the significance of openly acknowledging their team members. During DSG's earlier days in Philadelphia, Judee organized summer family picnics featuring softball games for all employees, along with annual holiday gatherings aimed at fostering deeper connections with her team and expressing gratitude for their efforts. Demonstrating kindness and genuine interest in every individual within your organization is a seemingly simple yet profoundly impactful gesture that can significantly boost morale. By reinforcing this kindness and interest with opportunities, rewards, recognition, and support, a workplace culture can transcend from good to exceptional. Sustaining this culture of care over time can serve as a driving force behind a company's enduring success for decades to come.

There's a scene in the movie *Glory* that affected me deeply. If you haven't seen the film, it's a Civil War story about how Colonel Robert Gould Shaw (Matthew Broderick's character) was offered command of one of the first all-Black US regiments, the 54th Massachusetts Infantry Regiment, and everything that followed under his command. The scene I'm thinking of is between Shaw and Morgan Freeman's character, John Rawlins. One of the Black soldiers was found trying to desert the unit, and Shaw has punished him severely. Rawlins explains that the supposed deserter was trying to find shoes for himself and the other soldiers. They'd been denied proper supplies, and their feet were torn up and painful because of it. They simply didn't have the fundamentals to go forward and fight.

Colonel Shaw, outraged, confronts the base's racist quartermaster and gets his men the shoes they need.[26] Which is the right thing to do, obviously, but I can't help thinking he would've done better, as a leader, to have noticed the problem himself. Taking care of your people means responding swiftly when an urgent need comes to light, but it also encompasses staying in tune and in touch with those people so you can prevent those needs from becoming urgent.

Not always possible. Leaders are constantly being pulled in a million different directions and don't always have the bandwidth to anticipate issues before they bubble up. But caring for our people means checking in with them, asking for updates, giving them ample opportunities to voice any rising concerns. The best leaders make sure every single person on their team has the tools, training, and support they need to succeed. No one goes without shoes. Ever.

And, amazingly, I've had a very personal experience making sure my people never went without shoes. Or in this case, boots.

I mentioned earlier that right after the September 11 attacks, I was helping to run logistics and supplies for my army unit. Part of our unit was preparing to be deployed, which meant we had to get everyone outfitted and equipped in desert-appropriate uniforms. And my team and I were struggling to find boots to fit one of the soldiers slated for deployment. Her feet were on the smaller side, and most of the boots we had on hand were men's sizes. The world wasn't quite as reliant on internet-ordering as it is today, so we were really scrambling and the clock was ticking. I remember thinking, *I can't send this soldier into the unknown without something as*

---

[26] https://www.youtube.com/watch?v=fLRpACNsqkk

foundational as boots—the part of the uniform that literally grounds you.

So I joined forces with an awesome sergeant first class with whom I worked closely in managing logistics for our battalion, and by some miracle, we found and sourced a pair in the right size.

Naturally, Murphy's Law kicked in, and the boots arrived on the exact day she was gearing up for action. During the pre-deployment phase, there are distinct stages for interacting with those slated to head out. The process for soldiers encompasses numerous phases, including medical assessments, equipment preparation, and specialized training for both individuals and units, all before they even step foot on the tarmac, making access seemingly impossible. Despite the protocol discouraging interruptions during the boarding process, my determination to deliver the boots to the soldier remained unwavering. While I can neither confirm nor deny, it's possible that a few of us jumped into a Humvee and made our way to the airfield where the soldiers were preparing to board, all to ensure the delivery of that lone pair of boots.

I distinctly recall sprinting across the airstrip, locating my soldier amidst the hustle, and handing over the boots. I'm fairly certain I received an earful from some colonel or lieutenant colonel in the midst of it all.

But then one of the general officers called me over. As I was running back to the Humvee, he snapped, "Get over here." And I did, obviously.

He asked, "What did you just do?"

And I told him. I said, "I'm sorry, sir, but she needs her boots. She needs those boots before she deploys!"

And he said, "OK, come with me."

I followed him, thinking I was in a world of trouble. But then he said, "Stand next to me right now." Which I did. And he put me in line with him to shake every soldier's hand as they went to board the plane. And when everyone was on board, he looked at me, handed me one of his military coins, and said, "Remember: people first."

I thought a lot about that experience during the pandemic, a time when putting people first really meant meeting them wherever they were. Everyone was frightened, unsure, facing down a whole slew of unknowns. Being a leader in that time period required a lot of flexibility, listening skills, and willingness to make big changes very quickly. Compassion and showing people how much they're valued became vital during that time too. The leaders who were laser-focused on doing the right thing for their people were the ones who weathered the pandemic best. They made it clear that they'd care for their people even when circumstances were truly dire. And that they would make the accommodations necessary to help them navigate both their personal and professional responsibilities.

This is simply the human side of leadership. Hubert Joly, former chairman and CEO of Best Buy, writes about what he calls "human magic." He describes this as a supportive culture where people are eager to express their untapped individual and collective potential, an environment where "everyone can become the best, biggest, most beautiful version of themselves." It's a remarkable mindset shift, and Joly also provides a six-part framework for putting it into practice. The element of "human magic" that struck me as timely during and after lockdown was authentic human connection. "Authentic human connections start with treating and valuing everyone as an individual and making sure everyone feels they belong," Joly writes. "The COVID-19 pandemic has highlighted how essential it is to see employees as individuals with unique talents, needs, and challenges."[27]

This is a tall order, but one that's essential in this post-pandemic world. A decade or more ago, this perspective might have been considered weak or ineffective, but today's leaders are evolving and accepting it. People no longer tolerate hierarchies where they are seen by their higher-ups as nameless, faceless masses, and the leaders who invest in meeting, knowing, and appreciating their teams are the ones who retain the best talent. *And* create lasting prosperity for their organizations.

As a leader, showing you care can take near-infinite forms. But no leader should be above driving a single pair of boots out onto an airstrip if that's what a team member needs to be successful.

Judee: I love that the general recognized what was happening, and that the choice you'd made was an important one.

Aileen: I'll never forget it. That was an amazing and impactful moment in my career.

Judee: And another concrete way to show people you care. You really stuck your neck out to make sure that soldier had what she needed, and while I know you never told anyone that story, I'm sure word got out, and I bet the rest of your unit recognized

---

[27] https://hbr.org/2022/01/
the-secret-ingredient-of-thriving-companies-human-magic

that. People always notice when a leader follows up words with actions.

Aileen: Speaking of actions, I think generosity is a quality that is too rare, and you, Judee, have led with exceptional generosity of spirit. You've built a culture of generosity at our company, and you do so in your civic and personal life as well. And you don't look for recognition. In fact, I know you often prefer your generous and giving actions to be anonymous. But people feel it, and are loyal to you and to our company and your civic endeavors as a result.

Judee: I do that because I feel so lucky and blessed in my life and love sharing. Even with people I may never see again.

Aileen: Whenever we, as leaders, can use our experience or standing to be generous, we should do it.

Judee: And that includes leveraging whatever privileges we may have to help others. Including other leaders and other businesses, if we can.

Aileen: Exactly. So many business experts love to talk about people "pulling themselves up by the bootstraps." This mandate to be scrappy, chase your dream, fund your company through creativity and grit. But what that mandate doesn't acknowledge is that we don't all start from the same place; some people have huge advantages right from the get-go, and others face constant bias or hurdles. You can't pull yourself up by the bootstraps if you don't have any boots.

Judee: How did this become the footwear chapter?

Aileen: I don't know, but I'm rolling with it.

Judee: Fair enough. And I love that analogy, truly I do. Leaders should meet people where they're at. If they don't have boots, don't go barking about bootstraps. The conversation around equity is always evolving, but it needs to keep happening.

Aileen: Agreed. Always.

While I certainly believe that the best leaders know when to let their people struggle a little, I also think that leaders are essentially here to help. We've got all sorts of advantages and relationships and insights, and hopefully we've earned them all. But hoarding them is just ... wasteful. Leaders shouldn't be gatekeepers; we should be gate openers. We should share our experiences and facilitate making connections so those following us don't have to struggle as hard.

Whenever I meet someone new, I think about being of service to them. It's easy to approach someone and think, *How can they help me?* But I try to flip that and think, *How can I help them?* With clients and employees, this forges trust and connections. With individuals, especially younger people, it puts them at ease since they no longer have to find some subtly diplomatic way to ask me for a giant favor. And it also positions me to help them. Let them name what they need, what they're seeking, and see if I can show them how to get it!

Both Aileen and I know that a high tide lifts all boats. We like people to recognize the opportunities associated with that. And we love being the ones who try to help that high tide come in. There's so much abundance and wealth and opportunity in the world. Some people love to act like those things are finite resources, like sharing their good fortune will make it dwindle. But that's baloney. The more luck and privilege you get, the more of it you should share or give away.

One way to be Deliberately Different as a leader is to use your power to make the world a better place. And in the next chapter, we'll talk more about how to do just that.

Chapter 6

You're Not Given Power;
You Earn It!

We have both come to understand and believe that "command and control," "top down," and other hierarchical leadership styles don't work. So before we dive into this chapter on power, we want to be clear: power in leadership doesn't have to be autocratic. In the world today, it actually cannot be something that's wielded or feared. In fact, that leadership style is not only ineffective but destructive.

This is, in part, because the business leadership landscape is evolving, and anyone employing a top-down leadership style is getting some serious pushback. Modern leaders are expected to manage their power in less domineering ways. As leadership expert Simon Sinek wisely points out, "Strong leaders earn loyalty. Weak leaders demand it."[28] And he's absolutely right. But to leaders who came to power in earlier eras, this can feel like a paradigm shift.

---

[28] https://simonsinek.com/quotes/#all

In some cases, we're seeing some leaders abandoning the C-suite because of this shift. In other cases, they simply don't have the skills, resilience, or appetite to navigate the new, complex workplace and workforce expectations that arose after the pandemic. And some are just exhausted. In 2023, a record number of CEOs resigned from their positions. Research conducted by Challenger, Gray & Christmas, Inc. found that 1,914 top executives left their roles in 2023, marking a 55 percent increase from the previous year.[29] Deloitte reports that issues of stress, overwhelm, and fatigue are among the top causes for this mass exodus.[30]

Why are leaders so drained and depleted? Because employees, boards, and shareholders are increasingly eager, able, and empowered to question the leaders who guide their companies. Power dynamics have shifted and will continue to shift. Not just in business but everywhere. And leaders who are not adapting their management styles to reflect new workforce partnerships and dynamics are becoming increasingly obsolete.

Joseph Nye—the noted political scientist who taught us about "tri-sector athletes" back in Chapter 3—has written extensively about the effective use of power. Here's what he says:

> In essence, power is nothing more than the ability to affect others to get what you want, and that requires a set of tools. Some of these are tools of coercion or

---

[29] https://www.forbes.com/sites/julianhayesii/2024/02/26/the-great-ceo-resignation-of-2023-3-keys-to-improving-ceo-well-being/?sh=27c2e5c33809

[30] https://www2.deloitte.com/us/en/insights/topics/leadership/employee-wellness-in-the-corporate-workplace.html

payment, or hard power, and some are tools of attraction, or soft power. For individuals, charisma (emotional appeal), vision, and communication are key soft-power skills; for nations, soft power is embodied in their culture, values, and legitimate policies.

With the exception of the Dalai Lama and perhaps a few others, it's hard to think of anybody who has been able to lead using soft power alone. On the other hand, we often talk about hard power while forgetting that attraction is a very powerful tool. Ignoring it is a mistake.[31]

Nye goes on to say that a blend of hard and soft power leads to something called "smart power," which is arguably more effective than either hard or soft alone. We'd add that whatever type or blend of power you might choose for yourself, you'll need to prove yourself worthy of it. Whether you're leading a corporation, a nonprofit, or an early-stage startup, it's your responsibility to actively earn any power that someone in your position might hold. Your title, your previous accomplishments, and your expertise all give you a jump start, but credentials alone don't give you power. If you waltz into the boardroom or your next town hall assuming everyone will respect you, you'll be in for quite a shock.

Now more than ever, power does not come from title or position. Power has to be earned. And once earned, it needs to be used fairly and carefully.

Anyone who wants to lead must understand that power stems from a combination of mindsets, activities, choices, relationships,

---

[31] https://hbr.org/2008/11/smart-power

and values. It's not just one thing. And it's certainly not limited to the traditional examples that come to our minds: defeating a competitor, disrupting an industry, winning a game or contest. In fact, sometimes we exercise our power simply by standing up for ourselves or for others. Or both.

As an army veteran, I think a lot about the soldiers I was privileged enough to work alongside and to lead. My experience in the military taught me more lessons than I could possibly enumerate here, but some of the top ones include the importance of mission, collaboration, respect, ethics, preparation, and discipline. I learned these lessons both from my commanding officers and from lower-ranking soldiers, from participating and observing, from situations I sought out and those that showed up unexpectedly. Today, I make a point of dispelling stereotypes about soldiers and offering context around military service. And when I do so, I think of every single person I served with and those that continue to serve and will do so in the future.

Which is why the following story unfolded as it did.

I had just come back from my very first active training exercise as a platoon leader at Fort Irwin National Training Center in the Mojave Desert. The soldiers stationed there take on the role of an opposing force, and fight against the visiting troops. Together we run through a variety of challenging scenarios, many of which are close to real combat, and get instant feedback on the decisions we make. It was incredibly intense and taught me the meaning of the army saying "You train like you fight, and you fight like you train."

You're Not Given Power; You Earn It! 115

That first full active-duty training exercise with my overall unit also brought me so much closer to my soldiers; nothing bonds people like making it through a challenge as a team. I left the exercise feeling full of pride for what we'd accomplished together.

Once the exercise was over, I was able to take some leave and visit my family on the East Coast. I was having lunch with my dad at a tavern near a local golf course when a man he knew walked over to our table to greet us. My dad introduced us, we made a bit of small talk, and this man asked me what I did for a living.

"I'm a lieutenant in the US Army," I told him.

And instead of responding directly to me at all, he looked at my dad and said, "You let your daughter do that?"

Well, *that* hit a nerve. Not just for me, but for my dad, too.

"Sir, with all due respect, I couldn't be more honored to serve with my fellow soldiers and my commanding officers," I said. "And it's because of them that you have the privilege of being on the eighteenth hole without looking over your shoulder. So a 'thank you' would be nice."

The man sputtered a little and did thank me, while my dad smiled with pride and took it all in without saying a word.

I'm generally a pretty calm, respectful person. It takes a lot to get my hackles up. But in that moment, I chose to stand in my power as an army officer, as a woman, and as a citizen. First and foremost because I felt this man was denigrating the people with whom I served, people who had become part of my extended family. Also because biased, elitist remarks like that should be a thing of the past, and when they surface in the present, I want to have the courage to voice my opinion. Yes, I wanted to stand up for myself in that moment, but more than that, I wanted to stand up for all soldiers,

116   Deliberately Different

all women in the military, all people whose work and sacrifices are often glossed over or dismissed outright. I wanted to use what power I had to remind this gentleman to check himself about his stereotypes, hoping that he'd think twice about saying such things in the future to other servicepeople, other women leaders.

I learned a lot about myself in the army, but I learned a lot more about teamwork, relationships, and the importance of trust among colleagues. So whenever I talk about being a veteran, I talk about my platoon, my fellow soldiers, my inspirational commanding officers, the experiences we all had together. I recognize that some of our service members—especially those who have served over multiple deployments—struggle with post-traumatic stress, depression, and other mental health issues.[32] I would never downplay the challenges that military service can carry. But whenever someone speaks disparagingly or ignorantly about the armed forces, I will always step up. Because I owe that to them. We owe it to each other and we owe it to all those who serve.

Judee: I love that story, Aileen. We both get feisty when it comes to anyone speaking ill of the people we care about.

Aileen: We do. Whatever power I may have, I want to use it to stand up to that kind of misguided remark. And the ideas that fuel it.

Judee: I'm right there with you.

---

[32] https://pubmed.ncbi.nlm.nih.gov/34283458/

Aileen: I know you are. You've been challenging the status quo for five decades!

Judee: Both because the status quo needs challenging, especially around issues of equity and inclusion, and because I honestly think leaders should not be afraid to question, challenge, and sometimes create a little controversy now and then. You need to say what you honestly believe and be willing to deal with the consequences. Don't be afraid to take some risks. It's OK to be bold! Especially if you can do it in a way that draws attention to issues that really matter.

Aileen: You're definitely known for your courage around speaking out and speaking up. I speak up when I feel moved, but also try to use my relationships and influence to help lift up voices that might not be heard—draw attention to people working on the problems or inequities that need to be addressed.

Judee: Another great strategy for using your power for good. I'm all about leveraging connections. In business, community, politics ... I feel so lucky to have had the variety of relationships I have had, and I want to utilize them in the most productive way possible.

Aileen: I think you should say a bit more about that. I see your skill at connecting and nurturing relationships as a huge part of your unique power.

The leaders I admire most don't just earn their power internally—within their own companies or organizations—they earn it externally, too. In their communities, industries, other branches of government, even other states or nations! And they do it by listening, putting in real effort to learn about people, offering to help, being unafraid to speak up and speak out. By getting into the rooms where big decisions are being made and voicing their opinions.

Since my first big professional experiences took place in Washington, DC, my first set of leadership heroes were politicians. And believe me, no one knows how to develop and steward interpersonal relationships like senators could back in those days. Working in Senator Walter F. Mondale's office, I watched and learned from the best.

I saw how those legislators—people from both political parties—and diplomats are able to communicate with different people in different ways, which is critical since one communication style does *not* fit all. Mondale himself was a genius at influencing and persuasion, talking people over to his side without strong-arming them, and he did it by using two strategies. He listened intently and was never afraid to let people vent, but he always tried to follow up with ideas around *how to take action* on whatever was bugging them. And he also did his research on every single person he needed to win over so he could bring up specific points when he spoke with them. He understood that giving others credit for accomplishments is important and appreciated.

My own approach has come from trying to use some of those same strategies to build a network of smart, accomplished, generous, action-oriented people. I learned that to be successful in leading, you need to gain their trust and respect. And they can rely on *me* when they need absolutely anything I can provide. I make it very

You're Not Given Power; You Earn It!   119

clear to everyone I know that I'm not just willing but also eager to support them however I can.

Some of the people I think are important to our success are members of the press, because from the very early days of DSG, I've seen how the press can make or break a business. When I first bought out Distaffers and shifted the company toward placing women in full-time professional roles, we were lucky in that we did it at an opportune moment and got a lot of publicity. After the federal government passed the Equal Employment Opportunity Act of 1972, corporate America was *scrambling* to hire women and people of color. And we could help, so DSG got some great coverage! That made it possible for our little company to land our first big account with Fidelity Bank.

Ever since then, I've greatly respected the value of good publicity, and conversely, the harm of bad press. As an entrepreneur, I have always personally overseen this activity for that reason. You have to know how to talk to the press—including what to say and what to avoid—and figure out how to give them honest information. I truly believe that developing good relationships with reporters and editors is crucial in helping any leader ensure their story is told truthfully and well.

Now, that said, I am not above putting the best spin on things. I don't ever lie ... but I'm always sure to emphasize the positive and excitement about the future.

All of this—going after good press, building solid relationships, telling your story—falls under the category of being comfortable in the spotlight. Leaders who want to earn and keep their power can't stay behind the scenes or hide in the shadows. They can certainly share credit and earnings with their teams and colleagues, and they must. But they've got to be willing to be seen and heard as individuals. And as representatives of their organizations. I see far too many people hanging back and deflecting attention. I'm all for humility, but to lead effectively, you need to get recognition. The spotlight is your friend.

I just genuinely like people, and I know you need so many others to wish you well if you're going to be successful. I love learning people's stories. I'm always curious to hear about someone's lifelong passion, and stories from powerful people about how they got to where they are. I don't like being alone. I'd much rather be spending time with other people, shooting the breeze, picking their brains, finding out what makes them tick.

There are some successful leaders out there who rely heavily on ideas and tactics, but I'm of the opinion that the best leaders truly like people. And the people around them see that and sense it. It's tough to earn real power as a lone wolf, no matter how dazzling your ideas and tactics may be. If you want to make a real difference, you need to come off as the real deal, not as an opportunist and someone trying to get ahead. People see through that.

Aileen: You are a natural when it comes to conversation. I've seen you put jittery people at ease and disarm people who were gearing up for a fight. It's amazing.

Judee: Well, I love talking to people, even in challenging circumstances! In the South, we call that "the gift of gab," and I've got it in abundance. It can be both good and bad.

You're Not Given Power; You Earn It! 121

Aileen: I see the value of stepping into the spotlight. And I definitely agree that the next generation of leaders needs to focus on their human skills: self-awareness, curiosity, vulnerability, emotional intelligence (EQ). With a workforce and ecosystem that demands flexibility and acceptance, leaders really won't be able to wall themselves off from their teams. The ones who are open and compassionate, who really listen to people and take their input to heart, are the ones who will build welcoming cultures. Places where every single person can feel seen.

Judee: I think leaders with those qualities were always successful. It's just that now, after the pandemic and with social media and new ways of connecting, employees are actually demanding that leaders be more real, human, and flexible. They're no longer tolerating "command and control" power.

Aileen: So true.

Judee: Do you think the pendulum might swing too far in the other direction, Aileen? Is social media changing expectations of leaders in this new millennial and Gen-Z market? That leaders may end up feeling like they've been stripped and limited in their power and influence by their own people?

Aileen: I don't. I'm sure some already feel that way, but the ones who understand where this shift came from and why it's important will find ways to navigate it. They'll both listen to input and push back on it when necessary. Even before this, I saw people-centric leaders who knew that they'd occasionally have to make unpopular decisions. Including ones that led to layoffs or other tough changes. They know that being a compassionate leader doesn't always mean being nice or making the easy decisions; sometimes it means doing what's best for the business and its people.

Judee: And that's a tough position to be in. But you're right, the best of the best know how to walk the line.

Aileen: They also know that once their power has been earned, the best way to keep it is to use it wisely both within their own organizations and out in the community. I have so much respect for leaders who become connectors and advocates, the ones who want to use their positions to do the maximum amount of good in the world. We need more of this, and I'm proud that our team at DSG is working closely with mission-driven leaders.

Early in my executive search career, I had the privilege of meeting the incredible Frances Hesselbein. I wasn't fully aware of her impact at the time, but once I'd done a little research, I realized I'd been in the presence of true greatness—rubbing elbows with a woman who had earned her power and had chosen to use it to make the world a better place.

I found out she had served as the CEO of the Girl Scouts of the USA from 1976 to 1990, totally transforming the organization from one where mostly white girls learned "traditional" women's skills like cooking to one that attracted girls of color and offered programs in topics like telecommunications and marine biology.[33] Hesselbein also launched a leadership development institute alongside management expert Peter F. Drucker, co-edited thirty-five books in twenty-one languages, authored two amazing leadership books of her own, was included on *Fortune*'s list of the world's fifty greatest leaders, taught leadership at West Point, and was a recipient of the Presidential Medal of Freedom.[34] And her motto was "to serve is to live." (Can you see why I ended up admiring her so much?)

And those are just the career highlights! They don't even scratch the surface of what she accomplished in her lifetime. Frances Hesselbein truly changed how people think about leadership.

Through her work with the Girl Scouts, she proved that long-established, bureaucratic organizations can pivot and succeed. And can do so by being more inclusive, subverting leadership hierarchies, and offering valuable development opportunities to leaders. On Hesselbein's watch, the Girl Scouts tripled membership among Black people, Indigenous people, and people of color; began offering science, technology, engineering, and mathematics (STEM) programs; and added the Daisies (kindergarten and first graders).[35] She hired educators and artists to write four different Girl Scout handbooks reflecting the different cultural identities of the members.[36] She

---

[33] https://www.nytimes.com/2022/12/15/us/frances-hesselbein-dead.html

[34] https://www.hesselbeinforum.pitt.edu/about-us/memory-frances-hesselbein

[35] https://blog.girlscouts.org/2022/12/in-memoriam-frances-hesselbein-former.html

[36] https://www.diversitywoman.com/dr-frances-hesselbein-leading-with-a-purpose/

instituted "circular management," which put her not at the top but at the center of a hub of leaders, a style devised to include more people in decision-making.[37] Hesselbein expanded the organization's reach and impact at the same time, never watering down the Girl Scouts' mission. With the help of her great teams and driven by her endless stores of optimism, she gradually became one of the most influential and respected leaders in the world. She earned her power over decades of visionary work.

I absolutely love this quote about Hesselbein from renowned leadership expert and coach Marshall Goldsmith: "She was incredibly focused on the Girl Scouts' mission," he told the *New York Times*. "She came up with a model called 'Tradition With a Future.' The Girl Scouts weren't moving into the new world at all. She brought inclusivity and diversity, but she never put down or insulted the past."[38]

That's exactly the approach I take to heart, and I am so grateful for Frances's example, particularly in my role as CEO. Just like her, I'm trying to look forward to the future while always honoring the legacy that made the present possible. It's far easier to discard past ideas and accomplishments to pursue the new, but doing so is incredibly short-sighted. We can learn so much from the leaders who came before us, and Hesselbein knew that.

After retiring from the Girl Scouts in 1990, she and Drucker cofounded the Peter F. Drucker Foundation for Nonprofit Management, which is a truly cross-sector institution. It brings together nonprofit and corporate executives, military officers, leading thinkers, educators, and consultants to share their ideas and hone their

---

[37] https://www.washingtonpost.com/obituaries/2022/12/13/frances-hesselbein-girl-scouts-dead/?_pml=1

[38] https://www.nytimes.com/2022/12/15/us/frances-hesselbein-dead.html

skills. The nonprofit later changed its name to the Leader to Leader Institute, and then the Frances Hesselbein Leadership Institute.[39] The Institute's core values include fostering leadership grounded in "the passion to serve, the discipline to listen, the courage to question, and the spirit to include."[40] Such a balanced and admirable list.

Of course, a huge reason Hesselbein's work is near and dear to me is because I had the opportunity to meet her and see her in action. I learned later that she actively supported leadership development within the US Army. On top of teaching at West Point, she became a trusted mentor and counsel to numerous senior army leaders, including two army chiefs of staff. She created the Frances Hesselbein Student Leadership Program at the US Military Academy and US Air Force Academy, an annual intensive weeklong opportunity for high school students that has supported hundreds of military-connected student leaders.[41] But of all of her contributions, the initiative I'm most familiar with is a program she launched called the Generals in Transition Program.

Working through the Frances Hesselbein Leadership Institute, this program encouraged army general officers to consider post-military careers in the social sector. Having worked closely with the US Army over the years, Hesselbein saw that many transitioning general officers still felt a very strong mission orientation. So she helped create the Generals in Transition Program to help these individuals take their leadership forward into a new sector. Amazing, right? Here's this group of highly motivated, meticulously

---

[39] https://www.nytimes.com/2022/12/15/us/frances-hesselbein-dead.html

[40] https://hesselbeininstitute.org/about/index.html

[41] https://www.westpoint.edu/news/community-news/lifetime-of-selfless-service-the-nation

126   **Deliberately Different**

trained leaders stepping out of the military. What better way to support them *and* bolster the social sector than training them to lead nonprofits, school administrations, philanthropic organizations, or resource management institutions?

Generals in Transition included a series of quarterly meetings, all of which included a panel featuring social sector executives, a representative from one of the nation's top executive search firms, and general officers who had made this transition.[42] Early in my career, a partner I was working with could not attend one of the panel discussions and asked me to step in on his behalf. I loved the experience so much that, after that, I participated every quarter for several years running, sharing my perspective and advice with multiple cohorts. It was rewarding because it connected me back to the military community and their journeys. Generals in Transition has been sunsetted, but I know from personal experience that it had a huge impact on its participants. And that's all thanks to Hesselbein's foresight and determination to leverage her standing to help others.

Frances Hesselbein passed in 2022 at the age of 107, and I suspect she lived so long because she lived so fully. Witnessing this woman's energy and passion in person was utterly inspiring, as was learning how she chose to use her power and influence to help as many people as comprehensively as possible. When she died, so many luminaries came forward to say how much they'd admired her: CEOs, generals, heads of state, academics, nonprofit executives, artists, and others. Judee always says that one of her guidelines and goals as a leader is to make sure that everyone wishes her

---

[42] https://hesselbeininstitute.org/ourwork/iap/index.html

You're Not Given Power; You Earn It!   127

well; it certainly seems like everyone who met Frances Hesselbein wished her well.

And like both Judee and me, she always valued character and individuality.

"Over the years, one of the most positive signs I'm seeing is how many women out there see themselves as leaders, and they are functioning as enormously effective leaders," Hesselbein told Diversity Woman Media. "You don't hear one of them saying, 'I am a woman leader.' No, they are leaders who happen to be women. It's the quality and character of the leader that determines performance and results. All of us lead in our own way, and when we don't see ourselves as categories, we are far more effective."[43]

Judee: She was one of the greats, that's for sure.

Aileen: Absolutely. And someone who began earning her power early on, and just kept earning more as she learned and accomplished more. And Frances Hesselbein was a real servant leader. She always seemed like the tallest person in the room, even though she was barely more than five feet tall. And she never showed a hint of egotism.

Judee: That is so important! I've seen people who work so hard to earn their power, and yes, they're right to feel proud of their accomplishments ... but when the bragging starts,

---

[43] https://www.diversitywoman.com/
dr-frances-hesselbein-leading-with-a-purpose/

they're going to lose ground. Even if they don't lose the actual power itself, they're sure going to lose the respect of their colleagues.

Aileen: I've heard other leadership experts say that learning to own your achievements is important. Especially for women.

Judee: But there's a subtle, tasteful way to do that. Wait to be asked about your achievements instead of bringing them up on your own. And give credit to all the people who supported you in getting there. No leader is an island.

Aileen: Very true.

Judee: And I feel like the very best way to keep your power is to share it. Even give it away, when you can.

Aileen: Or, on a related note, you can use it to help others. Which reminds me, there's another piece to that story I shared in Chapter 4 about the Emerging MedTech Summit. And it involves a Super Bowl champion.

Judee: You're kidding me.

Aileen: I'm not. So get this: I'm up on stage with my shortened talk jotted down on my folded piece of paper, and I'm handed a microphone. But with the open bar, it's just chaos in that tent. So loud! I try to get everyone's attention, start my talk, but I'm getting drowned out. And there's this man sitting at a table toward the front of the stage, taking notes. I later realized it was Mike Singletary, who was a linebacker for the Chicago Bears when they won the Super Bowl in 1984 and then had a long career in coaching.

Judee: And he was taking notes?

Aileen: Wait, it gets better. He notices that the crowd isn't settling down, so he comes up to the podium and says to me, "Excuse me, ma'am. Do you mind?" and reaches out for the mic. Not knowing what else to do, I hand it to him, and he says, "Yo. Yo! YO!" Three times. There was sudden silence. And Mr. Singletary says, "This lady has some really important stuff to say. And all of you need to listen."

Judee: Wow!

Aileen: You could have heard a pin drop in that tent. So I gave my talk, as I mentioned earlier. And afterwards he gives me a half-hug, and then all these executives and investors come up to me to talk; I get invited to appear on a podcast; everyone assumes I must be somebody important. I make some great connections. And it might have gone very differently if Mr. Singletary hadn't leveraged his voice and his standing to help me out.

Judee: So wonderful. More leaders should aspire to do that. To use their power to get things done and support others when they need it.

Aileen: I've seen you live that out, for sure. The JVS Fund for Women is a great example of sharing power. Say a bit about that, Judee.

I'm not the first to say this and I won't be the last: money is power. It's not the most refined statement to make and many people resist the idea. But money is power, believe me. And I wish that people would talk about it more so it could become less taboo. When you get down to it, everybody really does care about money in one way or another. It is seen as a measure of success, and it enables you to have the ability to effect change and make meaningful, positive, supportive differences in people's lives.

That's one reason why I've always wanted people to make more money at DSG than they were going to make anywhere else. It's the reason I shared 40 percent of the company with the employees, knowing that it was the right thing to do. (Nothing speaks louder about appreciation than paychecks and bonuses.) And it's the reason why I started the JVS Fund.

Back in 2021, I contributed the personal funds, I pulled together an advisory board of women, and we started making a plan for how best to help local women entrepreneurs. I've always felt it was important to stay involved and do what I can to support good work in the local Philadelphia community as appreciation for what had been done for me. So we launched the JVS Philadelphia Fund for Women in August of 2021, and we decided to give outright grants to women entrepreneurs with two strings attached: they have to become involved in the community, and they must give back to help other women.

As I'm writing this, we've done three rounds of grants and are reviewing applications for the fourth round. So far, the JVS Fund has given fifteen grants for $50,000 apiece to women business owners to help them mature and grow their enterprises, and it's been an incredibly rewarding experience. Especially since we don't just hand them a check and wish them luck! Our grant recipients receive consulting and advisory services from our board members and people in our professional networks, and we connect them to whatever resources they need to accelerate their business growth. Money is one form of power, but connections are almost equally important. We provide both so they have the best shot at lasting success.

One of our 2023 recipients, a fabulous chemist and pharmaceutical expert named Mumbi Dunjwa, told us that the business advice she got was essential to the success of her natural haircare line, Naturaz. She worked with our very own Leslie Pickus Mazza, senior vice president of corporate development at DSG, and together they decided to attend a few trade shows to spread the word about Naturaz. At one of these, they met with executives from TJX, the parent company of Marshalls and TJ Maxx, and the meeting went beautifully. Dunjwa landed a contract to sell Naturaz in the company's US and Canadian stores, then focused on raising another million-dollar seed round to support that growth.[44]

"The TJX deal is a direct result of JVS Philadelphia Fund for Women stepping in and having faith in us," Dunjwa told the *Philadelphia Citizen.* "If you want to succeed in life, you have to surround yourself with successful people, and so other women would

_____
[44] https://thephiladelphiacitizen.org/
business-for-good-jvs-philadelphia-fund-for-women/

really benefit from tapping into this network of influential and successful women ... They are a strong support system."

Not to get all sappy on you, but that warms my heart. And she's just one of our grantees! This fund is designed to make this kind of impact on every woman who receives a grant. I feel like I got a lot of breaks throughout my career—some of them really good ones—but if I had a little money or access to capital sooner, things might have happened faster. Now, since I'm in a position to be the accelerator for other women, I'm going to do everything I can to help them speed up.

As mentioned earlier, JVS Philadelphia Fund for Women doesn't take equity, and we don't ask for anything in return except that they stay involved in their communities and help other women. Our board members and their colleagues have donated legal services, financial advice, marketing guidance, and more. Because I'm not the only one who sees the importance of reaching out to the smart, driven women in the generations coming up behind us.

Women-founded startups got 2 percent or less of venture capital funding invested in Europe and the United States in 2023.[45] That's abysmal. Money certainly isn't the only form of power, but it's a reliably flexible and effective one. Those of us fortunate enough to have earned money over the years, I feel, have an obligation to help other women achieve success and access to equal opportunities. It's a concrete way we can help them build a better future, for themselves and for all of us.

---

[45] https://www.weforum.org/agenda/2024/03/women-startups-vc-funding/

Epilogue

Being Deliberately Different: Leading into the Future

Judee: Now more than ever, it's important to understand and embrace the future. Simply working harder and hoping for a different outcome won't work. To be successful in this new era, you can't be stuck in the past and operating by the old rules.

Aileen: I completely agree! Leaders must embrace new skills and ways of operating. So much of what we've been discussing in this book is about the human skills—human intelligence, so to speak, as well as societal acumen.

Judee: We're not suggesting that we throw out the window everything that made the last generation's leaders successful. There are timeless qualities that are still essential to the foundation of impactful leadership—the ability to attract great talent, have strong self-esteem, take strategic risks, communicate clearly, and structure operational and financial resources for best results. So when you think about how our industry and the next generation of leaders will evolve, what comes to mind? Cultivating new leaders isn't just about finding the right person for the job right now; it's about making sure the person you choose can lead the organization into the future. And that future seems to be changing awfully fast these days.

Aileen: And faster all the time. I completely agree, both in terms of technology and cultural expectations. Every organization we work with is wrestling with the issue of finding leaders who can navigate the monumental shifts in society, the economy, and technology along with the changing expectations of their employees, shareholders, and communities. Thanks to you, our firm has always been focused on identifying, developing, and advising leaders who are *deliberately different*. Next-generation leaders (regardless of age) are always "leaning in" to the future. They bring new perspectives, a sense of curiosity, a passion for learning, and multidimensional experiences, time and again, to move organizations forward.

Judee: At the same time, we know that people want progress, and want to be with organizations that are growing and are successful, but they don't particularly like change. Effective leaders know how to bring about necessary change without disruption. The best leaders are always evolving, and looking around every corner for what is needed going forward, rather than just relying on successful strategies from the past. Most importantly, though, leaders need to be inspiring, energetic,

Being Deliberately Different: Leading into the Future

and seen as contributors—whether bringing in business, doing mergers and acquisitions, or attracting new and impressive leadership. At the end of the day, they recognize they can't do it alone. They need thought partners and ...

Aileen: Exactly! That's why we've been successful in this business for five decades. Leaders rely on collecting the best advice and insights from knowledgeable thought partners. That is definitely in our DNA!

At the very beginning of this book, we talked about the profound changes we are all experiencing in this unpredictable, swiftly evolving world. Now we've come full circle to revisit this theme since there's no planning for the future without understanding the present and the past. Even seasoned leaders with varied backgrounds are struggling to anticipate what might come next in this dynamic environment. Whether they work in finance, manufacturing, private equity, academia, social impact, healthcare, or government, or really any industry that's impacted by technology and talent, they're hard-pressed to predict what new shifts might force unexpected pivots.

We believe that the world is at a critical inflection point, which is creating a sea change in leadership. The world economy, the state of democracy, shifting demographics, the direction of major organizations, and the flow of culture are all in flux. In their recent book *The Prepared Leader*, Erika James and Lynn Perry Wooten talk about prepared leadership as "your fourth bottom line."

One of the best ways for companies and organizations to manage risk is to be strategic and creative, particularly around succession planning. Preparing for leadership transitions must become part of every organization's strategic plan. Regardless of *how* various organizations approach succession planning, they share the *why*: they know that an uncertain world is best navigated through preparation, foresight, and purpose. Transparency and clarity of purpose need to be at the top of the list.

That can mean preparing internally for succession, or looking externally for candidates who can bring new insights and qualities to an organization. There are advantages to either strategy.

Judee: In our own case, it was actually both! You came from outside the firm, and on the inside, we have worked closely together as you transitioned into the role of CEO. And we learned a lot from each other, right?!

Aileen: We sure have! We don't always agree—in fact, we can really disagree with each other. Remember the Uber driver who was laughing out loud at our bickering? But seriously, it's been great for me—to have the chance to learn from you on the job, and come to know you personally. I understand the history, the people, and the nuances of our business far better than I would have been able to learn on my own. And as you said in the beginning of the book, your colleagues are your family, and I feel that way about you.

Being Deliberately Different: Leading into the Future   137

Leaders who are counseled and taught by their own predecessors are often better set up for success. They have the advantage of understanding the internal culture, politics, client relationships, future plans, and other nuances of their organization. But sometimes that's either not an option or else it's not the best option.

In the current environment, there can be a lot of value and even necessity for going outside of your institution for new leadership. Given the changing demands for leaders today, it's not surprising that there are unprecedented numbers of CEOs resigning. Research indicates these leaders feel burned out and overwhelmed by the dynamics and expectations of a post-pandemic world.

Leaders are experiencing new environmental pressures that most of them haven't been trained to manage or lead through. Their constituencies are being defined more broadly, and leaders have higher expectations to communicate more authentically and create an environment of belonging both internally and externally. They are often put under a microscope—any misstep or stumble is placed under heightened scrutiny, and you are potentially one click away from being canceled. It is easy to be the critic and more difficult to be in the arena.

But the effective leaders realize that, now more than ever, employees are craving connection and community. They want to belong and contribute to something important. And they want their employers to provide the setting and guidance they need to make those contributions. It's not always easy to be in the arena—but we need leadership who is willing to do so, more than ever.

This is why a new approach to leadership is *so* important right now. We know that the era of command-and-control, top-down, and other hierarchical leadership has passed.

The qualities we talked about in Chapters 1 through 6 are critical for new-world leaders, regardless of industry. People increasingly require their workplaces and leaders to help them feel anchored amid all the uncertainty and change taking place in this era. They need to feel valued, feel safe, and believe that they're putting their energy toward worthwhile endeavors.

When the next wave of leaders is successful at infusing their companies with genuine connection, they'll see tangible and ongoing benefits. Loyalty and reduced turnover are just the tip of the iceberg. A recent study by RedThread Research found that more-connected organizations were 5.4 times more likely to be agile in the face of change and 3.2 times more likely to have satisfied customers than their less-connected competitor companies.[46] And according to a study by Deloitte Consulting, when employees feel like they belong, it can lead to a 56 percent increase in job performance and a 50 percent reduction in turnover risk.[47]

Community isn't just a nice-to-have; it's essential for sustainable business success for both employees and leaders. Leadership can be a lonely role, and leaders need a sense of community just as much as their colleagues do. Building connection through collaboration, active engagement, and convenings—*not* through command and control—is imperative. A top-down mandate to create community within an organization is going to have the reverse effect: it'll spark dissonance and discomfort. Leaders need to create an environment of trust, encourage diverse perspectives,

---

[46] https://www.reworked.co/employee-experience/employees-crave-connection-heres-how-to-build-it/

[47] https://www2.deloitte.com/us/en/blog/human-capital-blog/2021/what-is-belonging-in-the-workplace.html

Being Deliberately Different: Leading into the Future   139

and offer honest feedback. Of course, building community is far easier when a leader is already familiar with an organization and its culture, which is another reason that developing a slate of leaders with the potential for succession in existing and yet-to-be-determined roles is so wise. Building that leadership pipeline now will help ease the transition later.

Leadership today is about future-proofing an organization, and the future demands connection. In *Punished by Rewards: The Trouble with Gold Stars, Incentive Plans, A's, Praise, and Other Bribes*, Alfie Kohn writes, "People will typically be more enthusiastic where they feel a sense of belonging and see themselves as part of a community than they will in a workplace in which each person is left to [their] own devices."[48] He's spot-on. Across my experiences in the army, at the Department of Defense, and in the world of corporate leadership, I've seen this truth play out again and again.

People at all levels are increasingly motivated to leave companies that don't meet their needs. To plan for a future that encompasses loyalty, talent retention, and leadership stability, organizations must embrace the importance of building community. Done well, it can pave the way for a consistently people-first culture that supports ongoing success.

Now let's talk more about new leadership from the outside. Increasingly, we are seeing executives being appointed who come from nontraditional paths, often from different industries and with different skill sets.

---

[48] https://www.octanner.com/
global-culture-report/2023-workplace-community

Judee: You know, some of the best C-suite leaders I know are the ones that have come to their roles by unusual paths. Instead of getting promoted from president or COO, they may have gotten started in marketing or HR and risen to the top from there. Or spent time working in a completely different business sector.

Aileen: I've noticed that too. Like Mary Dillon who went from being CEO at Ulta Beauty to taking the top spot at Foot Locker. Or Brian Cornell, who served as the chief marketing officer of Safeway before becoming CEO for a string of prominent retailers, including Target. It's great to see companies becoming more open to a variety of experiences as they move through succession planning. Leaders with multiple perspectives.

Judee: Absolutely. It's not a completely new trend, and it's actually how I started this firm fifty years ago—by finding leaders (particularly women) in nonprofits who could assume leadership roles in healthcare. But we're seeing more companies embracing executives who have had less conventional career trajectories. They're recognizing that industry-specific skills aren't as important as the broader leadership traits and values that we've talked about in the previous chapters.

Aileen: Yes, and given that the world today is about as far from static as it can possibly be, and increasingly complex, it makes

Being Deliberately Different: Leading into the Future   141

sense. Leaders who are adaptable, flexible, and can transfer their expertise across different environments are the ones who will thrive today. Often, those leaders are the ones who move across roles and sectors.

Judee: They're the ones who ask questions. If they're new to the industry, they want to understand the systems and structures, so they get curious.

Aileen: Exactly! And without preconceived ideas, that curiosity allows them to learn in a really open and beneficial way.

Judee: Just like you did when you moved from your policy work into the private sector, right?

Aileen: And Judee, just like you did when you moved from government to the private sector! During my transition, I had to keep a beginner's mindset. And it was humbling but also effective. When you're brand-new to a role or a sector, you need to ask a lot of questions—even ones that might seem embarrassing to insiders. As long as you go in with a willingness to adapt and learn, it doesn't matter where you came from. It's more about where you're going, and making connections that allow you to bring people along with you.

Judee: And, to me, that means grounding yourself in values. A gifted C-suite leader can come from sales or HR, leap from retail to finance. Where they got their start doesn't really matter. And none of that previous experience is a mark against them if they have the right core values and people skills. Succession planning is a waste if it doesn't revolve around finding leaders who share the company's values and will continue to live them out as the company evolves and grows.

Aileen: Right. Because when leaders disconnect growth from values, it's their people and their performance who are adversely affected.

Judee likes to say that at our firm, our assets, go up and down on the elevator every day. People are our greatest assets and are core to our business success. We are a service business, but this should be true for any industry. If you don't have engaged employees who believe in your business and contribute positively to your culture, then it will negatively affect your clients, customers, shareholders, and other key constituencies. Aileen's people-first philosophy supports that idea, and she continues to counsel leaders to focus on respecting, valuing, and listening to their people. Always.

We do this because we see people as the key element of the bigger picture. Leadership isn't just about your company or your individual career. If you don't leverage your position and power to do the maximum amount of good for the maximum number of people, you're ignoring one of your greatest assets—and a crucial component of true leadership. Companies can't just make record profits for themselves; they also need to be focused on doing right by their people.

That can take the form of things like profit-sharing, pay raises, generous benefits, bonuses, and other monetary incentives. But it

Being Deliberately Different: Leading into the Future   143

can also mean building or reshaping companies to better suit the people who work there and meet their shifting needs. The best and brightest leaders of the future will work to build a community where their people feel meaningfully engaged and that they are contributing to something larger than themselves.

This is what Simon Sinek refers to as the essential "why" that creates loyalty, inspires action, and drives success in any institution. When people understand their "why," they'll listen and adapt their leadership styles, leveraging self-reflection and seeking frequent, honest feedback. They'll recognize and accept that emotional intelligence is key to their own success. They'll make sure their organizations are welcoming, accepting, flexible, and adaptable places built on greater transparency and imbued with trust.

The future of leadership is in the hands of those who understand and value people. With the pandemic, the war for talent, the acceleration of technology, and the ever-increasing complexity of the world, many of us have forgotten how to fundamentally connect with each other. The best leaders can be Deliberately Different by being adept at building connection, communication, and community. They actively cultivate meaningful relationships internally and externally. They actively seek exposure to a broad and eclectic group of perspectives, and then bring those perspectives back to their companies and their people, which creates innovation and growth.

Over time, we as a society have become increasingly siloed and comfortable in our echo chambers. We no longer move in circles where people from a variety of backgrounds, generations, and life experiences congregate. We no longer seek or value community, and we struggle to accept viewpoints that differ from our own. Homogeneous environments can become stagnant.

Deliberately Different

Deliberately Different leaders will define the future. They are the ones who see the world not in linear terms but in mosaics. They cultivate relationships across a broad range of industries and sectors. With much deeper and wider perspectives, these leaders can see larger trends, sense impending challenges and opportunities, and react more adeptly than others who have more limited exposure.

We believe that while a handful of leadership traits have remained essential across time, the most successful leaders of the future will be transformational. When leaders own their strengths, embrace challenges, and take strategic risks, they are drawing upon the legacy of leadership built for them by great visionaries and innovators who came before. When they are more attuned to their environments, value and put their people first, lead with purpose, and know that they need to *earn* their power, they are shaping the future that is upon us.

The leaders who are Deliberately Different are the ones who are the most fulfilled, have a strong sense of purpose and a desire to excel, and will build a better future for everyone in this ever-changing world.

Are you ready? The world needs you now, more than ever. So let's get going and lead, together.

Acknowledgments

JUDEE

I want to extend my deepest gratitude to my coauthor and our CEO, Aileen. She is a remarkable leader, and I have the utmost confidence in her as she guides our firm to even greater achievements. I believe our best stories and shared experiences lie ahead of us.

I owe an incredible debt of gratitude to the late former US senator and vice president Walter Mondale, my role model Helen Wilson, and all the great leaders who came before me. They taught me so much about leadership, but even more about life, integrity, character, and the value of relationships. Thank you.

To my beloved family: Clay, Roddy, Kevin, Ivy, Olivia, Shannon, Izzy, Josie, Fred, Audrey, Incy, Peter Jr., Holly, and the entire von Seldeneck clan—my life is enriched because I am a part of yours. I am also profoundly grateful for Dale Jones, Camilla Ploss, Margie Nolan, Steve Morreale, Leslie Mazza, and all my colleagues throughout the last fifty years. Working together has been the most rewarding professional experience of my life. Thank you for your friendship. Life is better together, and I look forward to sharing more joy and impact with you on the journey forward.

To all my friends and supporters along the way, thank you. To my pals who share my Southern roots, my friends in Washington, DC, and my ya-ya sisters of Philadelphia—thank you for your unwavering support and the many laughs along the way. A big thank you to our wonderful clients and talented candidates who have made and continue to make us look good.

I want to especially thank the City of Sisterly Love, Philadelphia, that gave us "roots and wings" fifty years ago. This is truly the city of opportunity, and I hope to see its spirit of innovation and community continue to flourish.

Thank you to the DSG Global team and community. I am incredibly proud of what we have created and what we continue to create. I truly believe we have built something very special together that hopefully will thrive another fifty years! There is no place like DSG. A special, heartfelt thank you to my DSG family and the enduring bonds of friendship that last a lifetime.

AILEEN

I'd like to extend my deepest gratitude to my coauthor and the founder and chair of DSG, Judee. You have been my mentor, friend, and trusted advisor. Without your guidance, many of the experiences shared in this book would not have been possible. Your story needed to be told, and in your selfless way, you brought me into this journey. You have broken barriers and paved the way for countless entrepreneurs, leaders, and women, and I am grateful for your

Acknowledgments

unwavering belief in me as your successor. Your passion for community, civic engagement, and philanthropy is a powerful example for all business leaders and shows us that we can do more, together.

My family has shaped my life in immeasurable ways, and I would not be the person I am without their enduring love and support. I am eternally grateful to my husband, Greg, whom I met on the first day of army officer training. He is my best friend and unwavering partner in life and in our careers. His love and dedication hold our family together and serve as a remarkable example for our daughters. My daughters continue to amaze and inspire me every day. They have transformed my world with their growth, curiosity, and unique paths. Watching them flourish fills me with immense pride and joy.

I am profoundly grateful to the rest of my family, beginning with my late Nana, the original Aileen, who encouraged me throughout my youth, has been a guiding light, and truly influenced my path and my perspective. To my parents, Aileen and Frank, who instilled the values of integrity and character in me. Their love, guidance, and steadfast support over the years mean more than words can express. I'm so grateful for all the driving, cheering from the sidelines (even in the pouring rain), and being a sounding board—even to this day! And to my younger brother, Greg, my original teammate, whose entrepreneurial spirit and drive continue to inspire me. And to my extended family, including Sue, Allan, Meg, Steve, Marianne, my nieces and nephews, and all our relatives, I treasure every holiday, visit, our time at the shore, and the moments we share as we pass on our family traditions.

I'm grateful to all my teachers and coaches for teaching me the importance of learning and the meaning of "the only way to truly fail is not to try." Throughout my career, I've been fortunate to work with some exceptional leaders who have taught me, coached me, mentored me, and sponsored me along the way. Their guidance and wisdom have been invaluable, and their influence has been pivotal in my journey.

To those I had the honor of serving with in the US Army—from ROTC to Fort Gordon and the First Cavalry Division—your camaraderie, resilience, and dedication have deeply influenced my understanding of leadership. I salute all our service members, past and present. I'd like to do a special shout-out to my teammates, friends, and colleagues, especially Mel, Tanya, Jen, Joy, Heidi, Amy, Jamey, the entire 13th Signal Battalion, and my HKS crew. Your support, collaboration, and friendship are deeply appreciated.

At the Department of Defense, on Capitol Hill, and beyond, I encountered numerous public servants and leaders—many of whom became friends—whose inspiration and service have left an indelible mark. Thank you for your service.

To ALL my DSG colleagues, Steve Morreale, our executive leadership team—both past and present. Your commitment to our clients and having impact through leadership is what makes a difference and drives our growth and evolution. A special thank you to Sandy Blackledge, who keeps me going every day.

Together we wish to thank our publishers, Myles and Naren from Amplify, and our patient ghostwriter, Sally McGraw. They have been extraordinary partners who helped us get this book out in record time. We also want to thank our colleagues, Heather

Acknowledgments   149

Campion and Leslie Newbold, without whom this book would not have been completed. This became a passion project for them, as it was for us.

DSG is a force in our industry, thanks to the steadfast support of our partners at Shoreview. They have been with us every step of the way as we have scaled the firm and continue to ensure our success.

We are indebted to our remarkable and very talented colleagues who inspire us every day with their dedication to making the world a better place by cultivating exceptional leaders for the future, each and every day.

To all the leaders who have shared their time and insights, paving the way for future leaders—thank you. And to all those who aspire to lead, the world needs you!

About the Authors

Judith M. von Seldeneck is the founder and chair of Diversified Search Group, headquartered in Philadelphia. A pioneer in the search industry, she has been identifying and placing senior-level executive talent around the country for more than four decades.

A born-and-bred North Carolinian, she began her career as an executive assistant to then-Senator Walter F. Mondale in Washington, DC. Her road into executive search commenced in the early 1970s when she bought into a small Philadelphia firm founded to find professional roles for women. Buying out her partners in 1974, over the next several decades von Seldeneck built Diversified Search into one of the top ten executive search firms in the nation.

During the course of her career, von Seldeneck has been recognized by the executive search industry as setting the standard for retained executive search and has been active on numerous public, private, and not-for-profit boards of directors. Some of these include Citizens Financial Group, Tasty Baking Company,

Teleflex Incorporated, CoreStates Financial Corporation, Meridian Bancorp, and AAA Mid-Atlantic. She has also served as chair for the Philadelphia chapter of the National Association of Corporate Directors (NACD). She formerly served on the Comcast NBCUniversal Joint Diversity Advisory Council and as chairperson of the Women's Advisory Council. She was also a founder of the Forum of Executive Women, the largest association of women business leaders in the Philadelphia region, and recently created the JVS Philadelphia Fund for Women, providing funding for women-owned startups and early-stage companies.

In 2022, she was included on the Forbes 50 Over 50 list, highlighting groundbreaking women who are making an impact and have achieved remarkable success in their careers. She has also received dozens of awards and honors recognizing her achievements both professionally and philanthropically. These include the William Penn Award, the highest honor bestowed by the business community of Greater Philadelphia; the Business Leader of the Year Award from Drexel University's LeBow College of Business; the Association of Executive Search Consultants' Eleanor H. Raynolds Award for excellence in executive search; being designated as one of *BusinessWeek*'s top fifty most influential executive recruiters in the world; and induction into the Philadelphia Business Hall of Fame. She is a global board member of AltoPartners. She was also the second woman chair of the Greater Philadelphia Chamber of Commerce, and the only two-time Lifetime Achievement Award winner from the Association of Executive Search Consultants.

in jvonseldeneck

About the Authors　　153

Aileen K. Alexander is the chief executive officer of Diversified Search Group, the largest woman-founded executive search firm in the world. Her responsibilities include oversight and management of the company. She previously served as vice chair, leading the firm's Global Corporate Practice. Aileen is a global board member of AltoPartners, a leading international alliance of executive search firms, with Diversified Search Group as the exclusive US partner.

Based in Philadelphia, Alexander is a recognized leader in the executive search and talent management industry, having led C-suite and board-level searches from large global corporations to high-growth entrepreneurial companies. She leverages her expertise in technology, cybersecurity, risk management, and succession planning to enable clients to achieve their purpose and strategic priorities. Alexander is committed to ensuring client service that is creative, nimble, and responsive—always centered on people first—and building diverse teams that drive innovation, growth, and inclusive cultures.

Prior to joining DSG, Alexander was a managing partner at Korn Ferry, where she co-launched and co-led the firm's Global Cybersecurity Practice. She had leadership responsibilities for Philadelphia and was also a member of the Technology Officers and Aerospace and Defense practices. She entered the industry with Heidrick & Struggles, in their Washington, DC, office.

Before embarking on her career in executive search, Aileen worked in international security and defense policy at the Department of Defense and the US House of Representatives. She is also a military veteran, having served as a captain in the US Army.

Alexander's distinguished career is marked by significant leadership and service roles. She is a member of the CEO Council for Growth at the Philadelphia Chamber of Commerce and serves on the Board of Directors for both the University City Science Center and the NACD's Philadelphia chapter. Additionally, she is a board member at her alma mater, Villa Joseph Marie High School in Holland, Pennsylvania.

Alexander's accomplishments have earned her numerous accolades, including the Women of Distinction Award, the Power 101 Award, and recognition as a Veterans of Influence in Business Honoree. Her expertise and thought leadership have been featured in prominent publications such as *Barron's, Bloomberg, Forbes*, and *Fortune.*

in aileen-alexander

Timeless *leadership.*

DSG | Global

DsgGlobalCo.com